An Olympic Summer

TRANSPORT FOR LONDON IN 1948

An Olympic Summer

TRANSPORT FOR LONDON IN 1948

Paul Collins

Acknowledgements

This book would not have been possible without the dedication of the late V. C. Jones. By talking both to Jack Law and John Meredith and peering intently into his images, I think that I have gained some insight into the photographer, a sample of whose life's work is showcased in these pages. I am also grateful to the following for their time and trouble in preparing this book: June Collins, Taisia Collins, Ray Cresswell and Brierley Printers, Nick Grant, Mellanie Hartland, Ian Allan Publishing Ltd, Jack Law; John Meredith, Jay Slater; Matthew Wharmby and Peter Waller.

Paul Collins
Stourbridge
August 2008

First published 2008

ISBN 978 0 7110 3309 2

Published by Ian Allan Publishing

an imprint of Ian Allan Publishing Ltd, Hersham, Surrey, KT12 4RG

Printed in England by Ian Allan Printing Ltd, Hersham, Surrey, KT12 4RG

Code: 0808/B1

Visit the Ian Allan Publishing website at www.ianallanpublishing.com

COVER

Olympics – Saturday 31 July 1948
London Transport provided the large number of buses needed for 'Official Transport' to and from Wembley Stadium by pressing into service surviving members of elderly classes in their dotage. 'Bluebird' LT1410, an AEC Renown new in 1932, would be withdrawn after the Games.

HALF-TITLE

Leicester — Sunday 27 June 1948
The Southern Counties Touring Society (SCTS) pose with Corporation officials in Blackbird Road, by its junction with Abbey Park Road, with the Great Central Railway running behind. The line along Blackbird Road linked Groby Road with Belgrave Road and opened on 27 June 1924. It closed on 13 March 1949, the rest of Leicester's tramway system following suit on 9 November.

OPPOSITE

Birmingham – Sunday 18 April 1948
Birmingham had the epitome of a large municipal tramway system: well-maintained tramcars running on radial routes. When V. C. Jones visited on Sunday 18 April 1948 he caught its tramway system on the eve of the first major route closures. Despite the trams' finite working life, the Corporation did not stint on their maintenance. Inside the repair works at Kyotts Lake Road, he caught car No 628 in for the fitting of a new design of rear light and attention to her power wiring. No 628 was withdrawn in October 1950 with the closure of the Washwood Heath, Alum Rock and Lozells routes and broken up in November. *V. C. Jones/IAL*

Introduction

In retrospect, 1948 can be seen as a turning point for the UK. Through the debris of war a new world and society began to emerge and the 'change' that had been in the air for a time began to become tangible. The year was also one in which the UK played host to the Olympic Games, so, as with all other host countries past and present, the eyes of the world were on the country.

What was the UK like during the two weeks in July and August that became the focus of so much attention? A glimpse can be gained through a series of photographs taken that year. The photographer, Victor (V.C.) Jones, was a transport enthusiast and used most of his spare time to travel around documenting the changes that were happening to public transport in the UK that year.

Trams were being withdrawn, new buses delivered and trolleybuses were soldiering on. Railways, canals and road transport had been nationalised and many services were being maintained by a ramshackle collection of aging vehicles. This was never truer than on the railways. The 'Big Four' railway companies – the Great Western, London & North Eastern, London, Midland & Scottish and Southern – formed exactly 25 years earlier, were merged to create British Railways. Transport by road and canal and public transport in London were also nationalised, and all were placed under the overall control of a British Transport Commission and operated by a number of Executives.

The following statistics serve to put some perspective on the task that lay ahead for public transport.

In 1948 97,048 London Transport staff were responsible for the following: -
• 8,669,365 miles of tram and trolleybus journeys carrying 91,171,850 passengers
• 17,338,515 miles of Underground railway journeys carrying 52,838,008 passengers
• 23,472,969 miles of bus and coach journeys carrying 202,979,405 passengers
On 1 January 1948 British Railways' inheritance was: -
• 685,058 staff
• 20,379 steam locomotives
• 20,431 electric, diesel and other locomotives
• 39,596 coaches
• 1,214,321 freight vehicles
• 79 steamships
These worked together to provide the following services in January 1948 alone: -
• 16,557,864 miles of passenger journeys
• 88,376,736 passenger journeys
• 10,338,111 miles of freight journeys
• 20,042,288 tons of freight carried
Finally, in the same period, 3,929 Inland Waterways staff facilitated the movement of 704,843 tons of freight.

In the process of recording the changes happening to public transport, V.C. Jones also recorded much detail of everyday life during the UK's most recent Olympic summer. Step back in time and see what he saw...

.

1948

From 60 years in the future, 1948 is seen as a year of change and innovation in which the seeds of some now familiar things were sown, and many political and social changes began. By 31 December 1948, people had witnessed or heard about: airline hijacks; Alcoholics Anonymous; Apartheid; the Berlin Airlift; the Big Bang theory; Big Brother; cable television; the Cold War; cybernetics; fast food; the Hell's Angels; holograms, human rights; the Kinsey Report; LP records; Morris Minor cars; the National Health Service; Nikon cameras; plastic Frisbees; Polaroid cameras; Porsche cars; the Reith Lectures; 'Scrabble'; the Transistor; TV news; Velcro; the World Council of Churches; the World Health Organisation and, curiously, 1984.

The war dominated UK life in 1948 – the consequences of six years' of conflict were ever present in shattered lives, buildings and communities. Prime Minister Clement Attlee's Labour Government swept to power under the slogan 'Let us face the future' on 26 July 1945 with a 145-seat majority and promises of social reform. 1948 would be Attlee's mid-term and the year when most of his major changes were introduced. Attlee's programme was costly and implemented against crippling debt to the USA incurred via the Lend-Lease Programme. Under this, the US provided the UK with war materials for about 10 cents on the dollar, with repayment over 50 years at 2% interest. It began on 11 March 1941 and ran until 2 September 1945. Effectively a loan, the sum 'borrowed' was £1,075 million. Repayment was sometimes deferred and the final payment – of $83.3 million (£42.5 million) – was only made on 29 December 2006.

Despite this life was not all doom-and-gloom in the UK during 1948. Inflation stood at 6.6%, unemployment at 2.1%, average weekly earnings were £6.90 and the basic state pension was £1.30. Popular spare time activities were pubs, dancing and films. Cinema admissions were 1,514,000,000 (against 156,560,402 in 2006), to 4,706 cinemas (against 697 with 3,440 screens in 2006). In most homes, radio was the sole medium. Only the southeast had television – 120,000 homes had a set – up from 15,000 when the BBC's Television Service resumed on 7 June 1946. Television didn't spread beyond the southeast until the Sutton Coldfield transmitter was commissioned on 17 December 1949.

The Cold War

Tension had long existed between the ideologies of the USA and the Soviet Union. Suppressed when they were wartime allies, it reappeared immediately the war ended. America wanted to establish US-friendly governments and open economic markets; the Soviets wanted to stave off

Clement Attlee was the Prime Minister of the United Kingdom between 1945 and 1951. His government undertook the nationalisation of major industries and created the National Health Service. *Getty*

the threat of invasion by continuing to occupy territory they had gained during the war. This set the scene for a 'war-free conflict', to which George Orwell applied the term 'Cold War' in his essay 'You and the Atomic Bomb' published in the London Tribune on 19 October 1945. In 1948, this ideological conflict became public in five centres.

In Europe there were moves to oppose the Soviet stance. On 22 January 1948, British Foreign Secretary Ernest Bevin proposed a Western Union between Britain, France and the Benelux countries. As a result the Treaty of Brussels was signed 17 March 1948 (a precursor to the North Atlantic Treaty, signed on 4 April 1949), establishing the North Atlantic Treaty Organisation (NATO). A more public sign of growing US/Soviet tension came on 1 February 1948 when the Soviet Union began to jam the 'Voice of America' broadcasts.

When the war in Europe ended on 8 May 1945, Allied forces were ranged around Berlin. Under the Potsdam Agreement of 2 August 1945, the city was to be divided into four zones. The French, American and British zones were surrounded by the Soviet one – setting the scene for Berlin to be the major focus of Cold War tension. On 7 March 1948, it was announced that Berlin's western sectors were to merge into an independent federal state. In response, on 1 April 1948, the Soviet-controlled government in what was to become East Germany set up a land blockade of West Berlin. The situation climaxed on 21 June 1948 when the Western Allies announced a new currency – the Deutsche Mark – for West Germany. The Soviets responded by blocking access to West Berlin; cutting off rail and road routes through Soviet-controlled territory. To counter this the Allies began to fly essential supplies in. The first plane landed on 26 June 1948 and this 'Berlin Airlift' lasted 321 days – until 12 May 1949. Berliners also protested against their Soviet oppressors, who retaliated. On 19 August 1948, Soviet troops fired at German demonstrators protesting against the blockade.

Elsewhere in Europe, the Soviets had more mixed fortunes. On 25 February 1948, the Communist Party seized control of Czechoslovakia – celebrated as 'Victorious February' – and installed a regime that lasted until the 'Velvet Revolution' in November 1989. However, in Yugoslavia on 28 June 1948, the Cominform Resolution introduced the Informbiro period and the beginning of a Soviet/Yugoslav split.

Both sides became embroiled in other conflicts throughout the Cold War. One began in 1948 – in Korea. At the end of the war, the Soviet Union accepted the Japanese surrender and controlled the area north of the 38th parallel, the United States controlling the south. Both countries withdrew their troops in 1948: the Americans beginning on 8 April 1948 and the Soviets finishing on 26 December 1948. Korea's two halves also formed separate governments: the Republic of Korea in the south on 15 August 1948, and Democratic People's Republic of Korea in the north on 9 September, making the 38th parallel an international border. The Soviet Union and the USA retained their allegiances and thus were drawn into the Korean War, which began on 25 June 1950.

International Affairs

At the end of the war, with the UK in financial straits, control slackened over its empire. The costs of administering the empire also rose with the threat of guerrilla wars. India had been promised Dominion status, like Australia, New Zealand, Canada and South Africa had gained in 1930. It became independent on 15 August 1947, the day after Pakistan was formed. This 'partitioning' of India resulted in communal riots across India and Pakistan, with millions of Muslims moving to Pakistan and millions of Hindus and Sikhs to India. However, as 1948 began, it was Burma that gained independence from the UK, on 4 January.

India was soon back in the headlines on 30 January 1948 when Indian pacifist and leader Mohandas Karamchand or 'Mahatma' (meaning Great Soul) Gandhi was murdered by a Hindu extremist. Less than a week later, on 4 February, Ceylon became independent within the British Commonwealth. On the mainland, matters deteriorated rapidly following the death, from a combination of tuberculosis and lung cancer, of Quaid-e-Azam Muhammad Ali Jinnah, the founder and first Governor General of Pakistan, on 11 September 1948. The following day the Indian Army invaded the State of Hyderabad to assist with damage control. Termed 'Operation Polo', this act led to the deaths of Hyderabadi Muslims estimated in the tens of thousands.

A number of international organisations were formed after the war, some of which grew out of the United Nations (UN), formed on 24 October 1945. The World Health Organization was one, established by the UN on 7 April 1948 and holding the first World Health Assembly in Geneva on 24 June. Initially, UN council meetings were peripatetic, the first being held in London, but a permanent base was needed. A site was chosen beside the East River in New York and the groundbreaking ceremony for the building was held there on 14 September 1948. On 10 December 1948, the UN General Assembly adopted the Universal Declaration of Human Rights. On 7 May 1948, the first Congress of Europe was held in The Hague – the guest of honour was Winston Churchill, and on 23 August 1948, the World Council of Churches was formally constituted.

Israel came into being during 1948. An Arab-Israeli War ensued, and on 9 April 1948, a massacre of about 120 Palestinian Arabs took place at Deir Yassin near Jerusalem. It was part of Operation Nachshon, an Israeli military offensive to end the siege of Jerusalem. On 14 May 1948, Israel was proclaimed an independent Jewish state, with Chaim Weizmann its first President. The following day, Egypt, Transjordan, Lebanon, Syria, Iraq and Saudi Arabia attacked Israel. The UN Security Council appointed the Swedish diplomat Count Folke Bernadotte of Wisborg as mediator, but on 17 September 1948, the Jewish group Lehi assassinated him. Against this background, the movement of Jews from Yemen to Israel, termed 'Operation Magic Carpet', began on 16 November 1948. On 28 December 1948, a member of the Muslim Brotherhood worsened the situation by assassinating the Egyptian Prime Minister Mahmud Fahmi Nokrashi.

A new term first appeared in South Africa in 1948. In the General Election on 26 May 1948, the National Party narrowly defeated the United Party forming a coalition with the Afrikaner Party (AP) under Daniel Francois Malan's leadership. It began immediately implementing 'Apartheid' (meaning 'separateness' in Afrikaans); legislation prohibited 'miscegenation' (mixed race marriage) and individuals were classified by race, a classification board being created to rule in questionable cases.

International civilian flight became increasingly popular after the war, with unexpected consequences. On 16 June 1948, three armed men hijacked Cathay Pacific *Miss Macao*. They shot the pilot and the plane crashed, only one of 27 people aboard surviving. It was the world's first airline hijack. Six weeks later, on 31 July 1948, New York International Airport (later renamed John F. Kennedy International Airport) was dedicated at Idlewild Field.

In the USA, 1948 was a presidential election year. Incumbent Harry S. Truman faced challenges from Thomas E. Dewey and Strom Thurmond. Up to the polls on 2 November 1948, the vote had looked very close. In the Chicago Daily Tribune offices typesetters were on strike and election news was slow coming in. Needing to go to press, duty staff gambled on the headline 'DEWEY DEFEATS TRUMAN'. Next day a delighted Truman was photographed with the paper – he'd won by 303 votes to Dewey's 189 and Thurmond's 39. On 12 November 1948, wartime reparations were exacted in Japan. Seven Japanese military and government officials were sentenced to death for their roles in World War 2 at an international war crimes tribunal in Tokyo.

Social Change

Central to Labour's manifesto was the nationalisation of major industries and utilities. They transferred to state control on 'Vesting' Days. This affected the coal industry on 1 January 1947, and exactly a year later for transport. The 'Big Four' railway companies – the Great Western, London & North Eastern, London, Midland & Scottish and Southern – formed exactly 25 years earlier, were merged to form British Railways. Transport by road and canal were also nationalised, and all were placed under the control of the British Transport Commission. Later, On 1 April 1948, the electricity industry was nationalised, followed on 1 May 1949 by the gas industry.

Reforms to health and social security were equally important to Labour. On 5 July 1948, the National Health Service came into being, overseen by Health Minister Aneurin Bevan. The same day both the National Insurance Act 1948 and the National Assistance Act 1948 came into effect, establishing the modern welfare state. The following day the Widow's Benefit was introduced. In its first year, the National Health Service cost £400 million and gave out 187,000,000 prescriptions and 5,250,000 pairs of glasses. Other social concerns were addressed on 15 July 1948 when the first UK chapter of Alcoholics Anonymous opened in London.

Multicultural society

Both in the USA and UK, moves were made towards the creation of multicultural societies. In the USA on 26 July 1948, President Truman ended segregation in the US Armed Forces. In the UK on 22 June 1948, the *Empire Windrush* brought the first of several hundred black immigrants from the Caribbean countries to Tilbury Docks near London – the start of multiculturalism in Britain. This trend was boosted on 31 December 1948 when the British Nationality Act granted passports to all Commonwealth Citizens.

Only in America?

In 1948, five events in the USA showed that where America leads the UK follows. On 1 January, many eyebrows were raised by the publication of the Kinsey Report, *Sexual Behaviour in the Human Male*. On 8 March, the US Supreme Court ruled that religious instruction in public schools violated the Constitution. A week or so later, on 17 March, the first Hell's Angels motorcycling club was formed in San Bernardino, California. On 15 August, CBS began broadcasting nightly 15-minute television newscasts, and on 20 December, brothers Richard and Maurice McDonald reopened their

The classic Morris Minor was launched on 20 September 1948. It was designed by Alec Issigonis, who would later design the Mini. Over 1.6 million Minors were produced. *Getty*

restaurant in San Bernardino, California with their 'New Self-Service System' – fast food was born.

Paranoia?

Finally, a particular form of paranoia was also born in 1948, and two new terms were coined in the process. On 3 December 1948, George Orwell (Eric Arthur Blair) sent his agent the manuscript of his latest novel. Originally entitled *1980*, the book had taken so long to finish, partly due to Orwell's poor health, that it was renamed first *1982*, and then *1984*; the latter being the last two digits in the year it was completed – reversed. It told of an all-controlling state, ruled by the all-seeing 'Big Brother.'

Information Technology

Wartime research into code breaking led to post-war research into Information Technology. Two seminal works were published in 1948. One was Norbert Wiener's *Cybernetics*, or *Control and Communication in the Animal and Machine*, which articulated the marriage of communication and control for a generation of engineers, systems theorists and technical enthusiasts of many kinds, helping to initiate a discourse and a worldview that is deeply embedded. In July 1948, an article entitled 'A Mathematical Theory of Communication' by Claude E. Shannon was published in the Bell System Technical Journal. One of the founding works of information theory, it laid out the basic elements of digital communication.

On 27 January 1948, IMB's Selective Sequence Electronic Calculator (SSEC) electromechanical computer ran a stored program. Built in 1946/47, it occupied a room in the new IBM Headquarters Building in Manhattan. It was the first to combine electronic computation with a stored program, and the first to operate on its own data. It used 12,000 vacuum tubes and 21,000 electromechanical relays. The SSEC was visible to pedestrians and inspired a generation of cartoonists to portray computers as wall-sized panels covered with flashing lights, meters, dials, switches, and spinning rolls of tape.

On 21 June 1948, the Manchester University Mark I prototype ran the first fully electronic stored programme. Written by Prof Tom Kilburn, it was to find the highest proper factor of any number – and took 52 minutes to run. In October 1948, IBM introduced the IBM 604 Electronic Calculating Punch – a calculator that could perform basic arithmetic functions, plus square roots, briskly – hundreds of times faster than electromechanical alternatives. Significantly, the 604 also used 'pluggable units'. Engineers could pull out a defective unit and plug in a replacement, reducing downtime. During the year, Western Union also manufactured 50,000 Deskfax machines in the USA for fax transmission. Finally, on 26 June 1948, William Shockley filed the original patent for the first bipolar junction transistor.

Science and Inventions

Many familiar scientific concepts and inventions began in 1948. Swiss engineer George de Mestral found cockleburs clinging to his jacket after a walk. Examining one under a microscope, he recognised the potential for a new type of fastener. By 1955, he had developed 'Velcro'. In Japan, optical company Nippon Kogaku K.K introduced their model 'I' – a 35mm SLR camera sold under the name 'Nikon'. It was a good year for 'imaging. In September 1948, physicist Dr Denis Gabor demonstrated a new optical imaging system called a 'hologram'. Another photographic innovation came on 26 November 1948 when the first Model 95 Polaroid Land camera was sold for $89.75.

In the merging fields of astronomy and physics, on 16 February 1948 astronomer Gerard Kuiper announced the discovery of Uranus's innermost moon, which he named 'Miranda'. On 1 April, scientists Ralph Alpher and George Gamow published the Alpher-Bethe-Gamow theory about the 'Big Bang' origins of the universe.

In June 1948, John Walson couldn't sell TV sets in Mahanoy City, USA. Lying in a valley, reception was poor, so he put an antenna atop a nearby mountain and fed the signal to his store. The clear signal impressed local residents and TV sales soared. Walson improved picture quality by using coaxial cable and 'boosters' (amplifiers) to offer what he termed Community Antenna Television (CATV) – giving birth to cable television.

Two motoring legends were born in 1948. On 8 June, the Porsche marque was revived, its 356 being the first sports car to bear the Porsche name. 'No 1' was road certified that month. In July, it won its first class victory at the Innsbruck Stadtrennen. The following month, on 12 August, production of Morris Minor cars began at Cowley in Oxfordshire.

The inventiveness about in 1948 was also reflected in the year's Nobel Prizes, announced on 4 November. The winners were:
- Physics – Patrick Maynard Stuart Blackett – for discoveries in the fields of nuclear physics and cosmic radiation.
- Chemistry – Arne Wilhelm Kaurin Tiselius – for his discoveries concerning the complex nature of the serum proteins.

- Medicine – Paul Hermann Müller – for his discovery of the high efficiency of DDT as a contact poison against several arthropods.
- Literature – Thomas Stearns Eliot – for his outstanding, pioneer contribution to present-day poetry.

Was it perhaps a reflection of the post-war climate that no prize for peace was awarded?

In the UK

In the UK, apart from the Olympics, 1948 was marked by a series of Royal events. On 26 April, King George VI and Queen Elizabeth celebrated their Silver Wedding, and on 14 November, Princess Elizabeth gave birth to the future Prince of Wales; christened Charles Philip Arthur George at 3.30pm on 15 December at Buckingham Palace.

Manchester United beat Blackpool 4-2 in the FA Cup Final on 24 April 1948. *Getty*

Echoes of 'things to come' were seen in May 1948, firstly at Heathrow Airport (opened for civilian use on 31 May 1946), which became an international airport with the landing of a Pan Am Constellation from New York; and secondly in Blackburn, where the killing of a three-year-old girl on 14 May led to the UK's first mass fingerprinting, involving more than 40,000 men in an attempt to find her murderer. Known as 'The Blackburn Baby Murderer', 22-year-old Peter Griffiths was convicted for the killing and hanged on 19 November.

Signs of an end to post-war austerity came on 25 July 1948 when flour 'came off the ration' – the first wartime rationing to cease – followed by the end of rationing on clothes (15 March 1949); canned and dried fruit, chocolate biscuits, treacle, syrup, jellies and mincemeat (19 May 1950); soap (9 September 1950); tea (3 October 1952); sweets (5 February 1953), sugar (27 September 1953), and all food (4 July 1954).

Domestic culture also took hesitant strides. On 18 September 1948, BBC Television transmitted Robert Barr's Germany Under Control, the first TV documentary film. Later, on 26 December 1948, the first Reith Lectures began – named after John Reith, the first Director General – they were entitled Authority and the Individual and given by philosopher Bertrand Russell.

Entertainment

Two familiar pastimes had their origins in 1948. In the USA, Walter Frederick Morrison developed the first plastic 'Frisbee' – which he termed the Flyin-Saucer – and the manufacturing rights to a game called Lexikon were bought by a lawyer called James Brunot, who sought to jazz it up a bit by changing its name – to 'Scrabble'. In cinemas, Warner Brothers showed the first colour newsreel – Tournament of Roses Parade and the Rose Bowl – from 5 January. Another form of home entertainment advanced, when on 18 June Columbia Records introduced the Long Playing record, which could hold up to 25 minutes of music on each side. Notable British films of the year were both historical adaptations, which fared very differently in the USA. David Lean's Oliver Twist, based on the Charles Dickens novel, premiered in London on 28 June 1948, but was banned for three years in the USA because of alleged anti-Semitism in Alec Guinness's depiction of Fagin. Meanwhile, Laurence Olivier's Hamlet opened in the USA on 29 September 1948 and became the first and only film version of a Shakespeare play to win Academy Awards for Best Picture and Best Actor, bringing Olivier his only Best Actor Oscar.

Sport

The 1948 Winter Olympics were held in St. Moritz, Switzerland, opening on 30 January and closing on 8 February – Great Britain did not ' trouble' the medal table. The Grand National was held on 20 March and won by Sheila's Cottage, ridden by Arthur Thompson, trained by Neville Crump at odds of 50/1. A week later, Cambridge won the University Boat Race by five lengths. At the FA Cup Final on 24 April, Manchester United beat Blackpool 4-2.

...and finally

The weather continues to fascinate people in the UK. These are the temperature and rainfall statistics for the middle of 1948:

1948	March	April	May	June	July	August
Temperature °C	7.3	7.8	9.9	12.3	14.3	13.6
Rainfall mm	64.0	68.2	66.4	107.2	68.2	137.7

During that period occurred the warmest night ever in Britain to date on 28 July 1948 when a temperature of 23°C (73.4°F) was recorded in London. Perhaps it was an omen, for on the following day the XIVth Olympiad of the Modern Era opened there.

The XIVth Olympiad of the Modern Era – London 1948

The Olympics that opened in London on 29 July 1948 were the XIVth games of the Modern Era, a distinction applied to those contests held from the revival of the spirit of the original Olympic tradition in Athens in March 1896.

The Ancient Olympics

Records of the ancient Olympic Games date from 776 BC. They were dedicated to the Olympian gods and staged on the ancient plains of Olympia in Greece. The Games continued for nearly twelve centuries, but gradually declined in importance as the Romans gained power in Greece. When Christianity became the official religion of the Roman Empire, the Olympic games were seen as a pagan festival and in discord with Christian ethics. Thus in 393 AD the emperor Theodosius I outlawed them. Despite this, a notion of the Olympic games as a pure form of sport - pitting different people against each other in competitions that relied purely upon their strength and skill- endured through history, ripe for revival.

Reviving the Tradition

Curiously perhaps, its first two revivals happened in the unlikely setting of rural England. In 1612, Robert Dover opened the first Cotswold Olimpicks in the village of Chipping Campden, establishing an annual sporting fair that honoured the ancient Greek games but through sports that included singlestick, wrestling, jumping in sacks, dancing and shin-kicking. The second revival came in the mid-19th century in the Shropshire village of Much Wenlock. The local doctor, William Penny Brookes, was looking for a way 'to promote the moral, physical and intellectual improvement of the inhabitants of the town and neighbourhood of Wenlock' and, in October 1850, staged the first of his 'Olympian Games'. As in Chipping Campden, the 'games' were a mixture of athletics plus traditional country sports such as quoits, football and cricket. Penny Brookes also formed The Wenlock Olympian Society, and the games became an annual event in the village each July. The 1851 event featured competitors from Wolverhampton and Birmingham and within a few years there were entrants from most parts of the country.

Meanwhile, in Greece, wealthy philanthropist Evangelos Zappas sponsored the revival of the first modern international Olympian games as part of a National Industry Exhibition. The games were held in an Athens city square in 1859. From Much Wenlock, William Penny Brookes sent £10 to be presented to the winner of an event. The Greek Committee decided to award the Wenlock prize to the winner of the 'Long' or 'Sevenfold' race. Another Olympic games was held in Athens in 1870. For these games Zappas paid for

An artist's impression depicting the arrival of the Olympic Torch at Wembley Stadium during the opening ceremony of the Games.
Getty

Lighting the Olympic Flame. *Getty*

Penny Brookes requested an Olympian prize from Greece. In response King George I sent a suitably inscribed silver cup, which was presented at the National Olympian Games held in Shrewsbury. This sparked the idea of reviving the Olympian Games in Greece for Penny Brookes, and in June 1881, the Greek newspaper Clio reported that 'Dr Brookes, this enthusiastic philistine is endeavouring to organise an International Olympian Festival, to be held in Athens'. However, the unstable political situation in Greece at the time meant nothing came of this.

The eventual revival of the Olympic Games came about through the efforts of a young French education reformer – Pierre de Frédy, Baron de Coubertin (1863-1937). Ever since losing the Franco-Prussian War (1870-71), France had been seeking reasons for its defeat. Some, including de Coubertin, felt that this had been due, at least in part, to the French education system spurning physical exercise in favour of intellectual study. As part of the Universal Exhibition in Paris in 1889, de Coubertin had been charged with organising an international conference on physical education. He canvassed opinion widely, and in 1888 established a monthly paper – La Revue Athlétique – to raise interest in different sports in France. One person to respond was William Penny Brookes. Thus it was in October 1890 that de Coubertin visited Much Wenlock and saw a meeting of the Wenlock Olympian Games arranged in his honour. The 81-year-old Penny Brookes shared his dream of an Olympic revival, an international games to be staged in Athens, with the 27-year old de Coubertin, who wrote in the December 1890 issue of La Revue Athlétique that 'If the Olympic Games that Modern Greece has not yet been able to revive still survives today, it is due, not to a Greek, but to Dr W P Brookes'.

The culmination of de Coubertin's work was a congress held in Paris between 16 and 23 June 1894, which was attended by delegates from 14 countries and to which many letters of support were sent. At the end of the congress an International Olympic Committee (IOC) was formed. The Games of the I Olympiad were held in Athens between 25 March and 3 April 1896. Sadly William Penny Brookes had died just four months earlier, in December 1895. His contribution was overlooked for many years, but in 1994, Juan Antonio Samaranch, President of the International Olympic Committee, made a pilgrimage to Much Wenlock. He said, 'I have come because this is where the modern Olympics started'. Samaranch also laid a wreath on Penny Brookes' grave at Holy Trinity Church. 'Dr Brookes was really the founder of the modern Olympics', he added.

the refurbishment of the ancient Olympic Panathenian stadium, which were used again in 1875, before being refurbished a second time and used for the 1896 Athens Games.

In 1865, William Penny Brookes helped to establish the National Olympian Association based in Liverpool. The aim was to provide a sports association for amateur athletes. Its first festival, held the following year at London's Crystal Palace, was a great success and attracted in excess of 10,000 spectators. The event became annual and for Queen Victoria's Jubilee in 1877

London 1948

London became the host city for the XIVth Olympiad by a roundabout route. In June 1939, the city had won the ballot to host the Games of the XIIIth Olympiad to be held in the summer of 1944, beating Athens, Budapest, Detroit, Helsinki, Lausanne, Montreal and Rome on the first ballot but, not for the first time, war intervened. Indeed, with hindsight, some of the choices for host city were a little 'unfortunate'. The 1916 Olympics were to have been held in Berlin, and the 1940 games were originally awarded to Tokyo. After Japan invaded China in 1938, the Japanese government ordered the organising committee to halt preparations after sixteen sites had been all but completed. The Summer Games were rewarded to Helsinki but were cancelled when Soviet troops invaded Finland in 1939. The 1944 Summer Games were cancelled by default but, by dint of being next in line, London was given the opportunity of hosting the 1948 Games without a ballot.

Preparation for the games

An organising committee was formed on 14 March 1946 from which a number of other committees and sub-committees were formed. Official invitations to take part in the games were issued to all the member countries of the IOC on 17 April 1947. Meanwhile decisions were being made on various aspects of the games' conduct and appearance, these included: -

- Restaging the torch relay – bringing the Olympic flame from Greece to the host nation by a relay of runners – first seen at the Munich Olympics in 1936;
- Restoring the IOC's ceremonial flag, last used in 1936 and found amongst the ruins of Berlin in 1945;
- Designing the games' symbol, which it was felt should be typically British, but with a special meaning. Eventually the clock tower of the Houses of Parliament was chosen, with Big Ben's hands at 4 o'clock – the time at which the games would be declared open.

Venues – not just London

Although the 1948 Olympics are usually described as being in London, the events were in fact hosted around the south east of England and far west in Torbay. The respective venues were:

Athletics (track and field) – Empire Stadium Wembley
Basketball – Harringay Arena
Boxing – Empress Hall, Earls Court (preliminary bouts);

Empire Pool, Wembley (main bouts)
Canoeing – Henley-on-Thames
Cycling – Herne Hill (track events); Windsor Great Park (road race)
Equestrian – Aldershot (main events); Empire Stadium (Prix des Nations)
Fencing – Former Palace of Engineering, Wembley Empire Exhibition site
Football – Empire Stadium Wembley
Gymnastics – Empire Stadium (transferred to Empress Hall, Earl's Court due to rain)
Hockey – Empire Stadium Wembley
Modern Pentathlon – Riding, Fencing, Swimming and Running around Aldershot; Shooting at Bisley
Rowing – Henley-on-Thames
Shooting – Bisley
Swimming – Finchley Pool (preliminary rounds); Empire Pool (main events)
Weightlifting – Empress Hall, Earls Court
Yachting – Torbay

Accommodation

In post-war austerity Britain, no Olympic Village was built. The male athletes were put up mainly at a number of military camps:
Ex-Military Camp, Richmond Park;
RAF Camps at Uxbridge and West Drayton;
Outside London:
Middlesex County Council Schools (Men); private establishments (Women). Athletes were also put up at schools and three Greater London colleges, including Southlands College, where most of the women athletes were housed. Between 25 and 30 sites were used, meaning that transport had to be arranged from there to the various sports grounds. Competitors in the equestrian events at Aldershot were housed at Sandhurst; those in the shooting at Bisley were accommodated in an on-site camp; rowers at Henley-on-Thames were housed in three schools in High Wycombe and the yachting teams were put up in local hotels in Torquay.

Catering

Flour rationing had ended in the UK just four days before the Olympic games opened but otherwise all other foodstuffs were still 'on the ration'. Given that rationing was not necessarily in operation in the home countries of the overseas competitors, the Ministry of Food was asked to grant an increased ration scale to all the athletes taking part in the games. It was decided that

The London 1948 commemorative medal on display. *Getty*

the athletes would be allocated a ration scale equivalent to that allowed for workers in heavy industry, which meant 5,467 calories a day, instead of the normal 2,600. Competing nations were notified of this in April 1948, and many brought additional food with them. Therefore, during the games, the food supplied to competitors came from a mixture of the:

• Special Olympic scale ration;
• Food brought by nations for their own consumption;
• Gift food donated by some nations for all to consume, and,
• Gift food donated by British firms or organisations.

Transport Arrangements

The Organising Committee's Transport Department was formed in July 1947. Its brief was to make arrangements for the movement of around 6,000 competitors between their accommodation and the various sporting venues over a period of 17 days. London Transport offered the use of some of its double-decker buses, but the number of vehicles available was limited because, owing to post-war shortages, they were hiring in up to 400 single-deck coaches a day to augment their fleet of 3,000 or so buses. Nonetheless, London Transport offered the use of up to twenty 56-seater double-deckers, twenty 30-seater single deck coaches and thirty 20-seater smaller coaches. The latter were of an obsolete type and were offered with reluctance owing to their age and condition. The only other major operator to offer its vehicles was the Aldershot & District Traction Co., who provided a similar service to London Transport's in connection with the equestrian events.

These special services began in 8 July 1948 and ran until 21 August. In that time a total distance of 345,000 miles was covered, mostly without incident. There were a few exceptions though. One double-decker went off-route in West Drayton and struck a low bridge; an excited cycle coach drove away a small eight-seat vehicle but badly damaged it in Windsor Park, and, in two separate incidents in London and Henley, competitors drove buses away.

The Opening Ceremony

The Games opened on 29 July 1948. As with the previous day, the weather was fine and the sun blazed down on the 85,000 people inside Wembley Stadium. Proceedings began at 14.00 and King George VI and Queen Elizabeth arrived at 14.45 to be seated for the march in of the teams from the participating countries. In total, 4,099 contestants from 59 nations took part. Compared with the previous games, the number of male competitors was down slightly, from 3,738 to 3,714, but the number of women increased

from 328 to 385. The countries held responsible for World War II, Germany and Japan, were excluded and the Soviet Union decided to abstain. The march in, which lasted for 50 minutes, was headed by Greece, with Great Britain, as the host nation, coming in last. This was followed by a speech from Lord Burghley, Chairman of the Organising Committee, which was redolent with references to the war and expressed the hope that, 'in the hearts of millions in every corner of the earth, that warm flame of hope, for a better understanding in the world which has burned so low, will flare up into a very beacon, pointing a way to the goal through the Fellowship of Sport'. He then asked the King to declare the games open. At 16.00 precisely, King George VI did so with the words, 'I proclaim open the Olympic Games of London celebrating the XIV Olympiad of the Modern Era'. The crowd cheered, and the (repaired) Olympic flag was struck atop a 35ft flagpole at the end of the arena. 2,500 pigeons were released and a 21-gun salute was fired.

At this point, the last runner in the Torch Relay – John Mark, a 22-year-old athlete from Surbiton, Surrey – entered the stadium. The sacred flame had been kindled in Greece on 17 July and had been carried by 762 runners on the 2,000-mile journey to London. Mark completed a circuit of the track, mounted the steps to the bowl where the flame was to be kindled, faced the stadium, held the torch high, turned and dipped it into the bowl, whereupon the sacred flame sprang into life. Thereafter, a dedicatory address by the Archbishop of York was followed by the swearing of the Olympic Oath, which was taken by Wing Commander Donald Finlay, captain of the British team. After the National Anthem, the teams paraded out of the stadium, again headed by Greece. Thus the games were opened. Later, between 1 and 2 August, a torch lit by the sacred flame in Wembley was carried by relay to Torre Abbey in Torquay, where a second flame was lit for the Olympic Regatta.

Highlights

Two athletes who were Olympic champions in the 1936 Games managed to defend their titles. They were Ilona Elek of Hungary in the women's foil fencing and Jan Brzak of Czechoslovakia in the canoeing Canadian pairs 1,000m. Fanny Blankers-Koen of the Netherlands emerged as the star of the 1948 Games. A 30-year-old mother of two, she won individual gold medals in the 100m and 200m dashes and the 80m hurdles, and won a fourth gold running the anchor leg on Holland's 400m relay team. In fact Blankers-Koen was the world record holder in six events. According to the rules of the day, she was only allowed to enter four, but she won them all.

At the other end of the track and field age spectrum was 17-year-old Bob Mathias. Just two months after graduating from high school in Tulare, California, Mathias was competing in only his third decathlon. He was third after the first day of competition, but he pulled into the lead with a tremendous discus throw on the second day and held on to win with a plodding but gutsy 5.11 in the concluding 1500m run.

The surprising winner in the men's 100m dash was Harrison 'Bones' Dillard of the United States. The world record holder in the 120-yard hurdles, Dillard failed to qualify in that event and barely made the team by finishing third in the 100m trials. He and team-mate Barney Ewell were both clocked in 10.3 seconds, tying the world record, but judges awarded Dillard the gold medal after studying the photo-finish results. (Incidentally, this was the first time that a photo-finish camera was used at the Olympics.) Dillard won a second gold as a member of the 400m relay team. Mel Patton, the winner of the 200m dash, also won gold in the relay. The only other double gold medallist in track and field was Mal Whitfield, who won the 800m run and ran the anchor leg on the 4 x 400m relay team. Whitfield also took a bronze in the 400m run.

Although there was no really dominant swimmer, the United States won all six men's events. Jimmy McLane, Wally Ris, and Bill Smith each won an individual gold medal and a second gold in the freestyle relay. Ann Curtis was the only individual gold medallist among American women, in the 400m freestyle, and she too added a second in the relay, swimming the anchor leg in an incredible 1min 04.4sec. That was nearly two seconds better than the winning time in the 100m freestyle, in which Curtis had finished second.

For the fifth straight time, Americans took gold medals in all four diving events, with Vicki Draves becoming the first woman to win both the springboard and the platform.

Concert pianist Micheline Ostermeyer of France won both the shot put and the discus throw. Karoly Takacs was a member of the Hungarian world champion pistol shooting team in 1938 when a grenade shattered his right hand – his pistol hand. Takacs taught himself to shoot with his left hand and, ten years later, he won an Olympic gold medal in the rapid-fire pistol event.

Stan Cox, seventh in a 10,000m won by the Czech who was to dominate for the next five years, Emil Zatopek, was only allowed two days off from his job – one for the opening ceremony, and one for the race. Cox was later told he should have been given fifth place as he had run an extra lap because the officials had been confused by Zatopek overtaking everyone. Veteran Finn, Heikki Savolainen was taking part in his fourth Olympics and was over

40 years old, but nonetheless he won a gold medal on the pommel horse.

A dramatic photo-finish in the London Olympics. *Getty*

Closing Ceremony
14 August 1948 from 18.00

Firsts
- Starting blocks – Introduction of blocks to facilitate the start for athletes in sprint races (100m to 400m).
- Photo finishes – photo-finish equipment, which was normally used for horseracing, and was only used to aid the judges to decide placings.
- Television coverage.

Something not widely known is that the Paralympic movement actually started in this country. At Stoke Mandeville Hospital in the 1940s, Sir Ludwig

Guttmann worked with war veterans who had suffered spinal injuries. He believed sport could aid their recovery. In 1948, at the same time as the London Olympics, he organised the first wheelchair Games. The event gained the official title of the Paralympic Games and was held to coincide with the 1960 and 1964 Olympics in Rome and Tokyo. Now both events always happen in the same year, and since 1988 they have used the same stadiums.

Lasts
• Games to use bamboo poles for the pole vault.

Costs
The estimated cost of staging the 2012 Olympics in London continues to rise. At the time of writing it stood at £3.3bn. This is in stark contrast to the costs of staging the Games in 1948. Then the total expenditure was a mere £732,000, which included the cost of housing, feeding and transporting the competitors whilst they were in the country, and to do all of this only 219 people were directly employed in running the games.

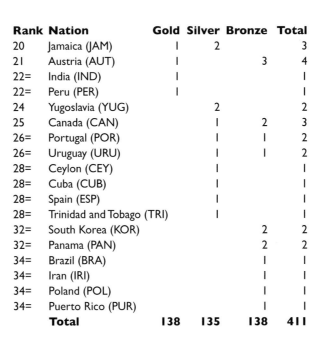

The opening ceremony of the 1948 London Olympics. *Getty*

Medal table

Rank	Nation	Gold	Silver	Bronze	Total
1	United States (USA)	38	27	19	84
2	Sweden (SWE)	16	11	17	44
3	France (FRA)	10	6	13	29
4	Hungary (HUN)	10	5	12	27
5	Italy (ITA)	8	11	8	27
6	Finland (FIN)	8	7	5	20
7	Turkey (TUR)	6	4	2	12
8	Czechoslovakia (TCH)	6	2	3	11
9	Switzerland (SUI)	5	10	5	20
10	Denmark (DEN)	5	7	8	20
11	Netherlands (NED)	5	2	9	16
12	Great Britain (GBR)	3	14	6	23
13	Argentina (ARG)	3	3	1	7
14	Australia (AUS)	2	6	5	13
15	Belgium (BEL)	2	2	3	7
16	Egypt (EGY)	2	2	1	5
17	Mexico (MEX)	2	1	2	5
18	South Africa (RSA)	2	1	1	4
19	Norway (NOR)	1	3	3	7

Rank	Nation	Gold	Silver	Bronze	Total
20	Jamaica (JAM)	1	2		3
21	Austria (AUT)	1		3	4
22=	India (IND)	1			1
22=	Peru (PER)	1			1
24	Yugoslavia (YUG)		2		2
25	Canada (CAN)		1	2	3
26=	Portugal (POR)		1	1	2
26=	Uruguay (URU)		1	1	2
28=	Ceylon (CEY)		1		1
28=	Cuba (CUB)		1		1
28=	Spain (ESP)		1		1
28=	Trinidad and Tobago (TRI)		1		1
32=	South Korea (KOR)			2	2
32=	Panama (PAN)			2	2
34=	Brazil (BRA)			1	1
34=	Iran (IRI)			1	1
34=	Poland (POL)			1	1
34=	Puerto Rico (PUR)			1	1
	Total	**138**	**135**	**138**	**411**

The photographer – Victor C. 'Vic' Jones

The following photographs are the work of V.C. Jones. Born c1916, he lived most of his life with his two sisters in a house in Tyneham Road, Battersea. After school he worked as a clerk for Allied Schools, a foundation which ran schools in the Felixstowe area. Like many at that time he suffered from tuberculosis, which left him weakened for the rest of his life. However, this did not weaken his spirit, and all those who knew him recall a witty and quick-witted character with a tendency to use awful puns.

Trams and buses were his great interest, and he has left two great legacies of these. One is through his work with Geoffrey Ashwell, Jack Law and John Meredith in recording the sounds of London's closing tramway system on tape; the other through his prodigious photography. For the latter he used a 35mm Leica camera, at a time when the format was far from popular and commonplace. Vic Jones never drove a car, but he was introduced to the joys of Vespa scooters by Jack Law, and quickly became a devotee. He died on 26 September 1981.

London – Saturday 13 March 1948

Elephant & Castle has long been an important junction – it was once known as 'the Piccadilly of South London'. Stane Street – a Roman road – was joined there by roads from Kent, Walworth and Kennington, and later by roads to London's new bridges. Heavy use by horse-drawn vehicles led blacksmith John Flaxman to set up a forge on an island between the roads in 1641. In the middle of the 18th century, his former 'smithy' became an inn and was renamed the Elephant & Castle.

The spirit of the Elephant and Castle was captured by Sue Hubbard, writing in *The Independent Review* on 21 April 2004 about a series of photographs taken there in 1948 by Bert Hardy for *Picture Post*: 'This was a London of bomb- and building-sites, of street markets and coal merchants, a cockney community that had essentially been untouched for generations, where children played in the street and escape from the hard grind of daily life was sought in the local pub. The faces are pinched and aged with hardship and deprivation... It is a world that Hogarth might have recognised. Elephant and Castle was one of the most heavily bombed areas of London. Life was harsh and grinding, but with its boxing and music halls, its jellied-eel stalls, thieves and good-time girls, it was a real community'.

On 13 March 'Feltham' No 2167 – the penultimate experimental car built for the Metropolitan Electric Tramways Co. – was working through on route 18, travelling in the same direction as crowds of people. As MET No 330 it had entered service on 6 November 1929, and been stored out of use for most of World War 2. Withdrawn in December 1949, No 2167 was cut up at Purley depot shortly afterwards. A few years later, the Elephant & Castle itself suffered a similar fate. Its comprehensive redevelopment was planned in 1955-6 and effected in the early 1960s when the Elephant & Castle Shopping Centre was built, the first of its kind in Europe. An ambitious regeneration project, planned by Southwark Council from June 2002, will, by 2014, see the area once again transformed.

London – Saturday 13 March 1948

From the top deck of a passing tram, V. C. Jones caught Class E/1r tramcar No 1386, working route 48 to West Norwood, drawing alongside broken-down STL2405, which had been headed to the same destination but was instead the focus of much attention, save for that of an unconcerned cyclist in the foreground. The use of a wheel brace suggests that a wheel had been changed or a tyre punctured. The bus was one of a batch of 327 Chiswick-built roofbox AEC Regents among the numerous and varied STL class. It carried posters for the *Daily Mail* Ideal Home Exhibition at Olympia, which had been opened on 2 March by King George VI and Queen Elizabeth, accompanied by Princess Margaret.

London – Tuesday 23 March 1948

V. C. Jones' work for Allied Schools meant that he was based in Central London and it seems that he took his camera to work with him. Perhaps on a lunch break, he paused on the Embankment and leaned against a wooden barrier next to a switch pillar opposite the southern portal of the Kingsway Subway, which emerged beneath Waterloo Bridge. The first Waterloo Bridge was designed by John Rennie and built between 1811 and 1817. Known as the Strand Bridge, in 1816 Parliament declared that its name would be Waterloo Bridge to commemorate Wellington's triumph over Napoleon. V C Jones lingered there for a few minutes to record a little of the everyday activity there that would, in just over four years' time, become history. First he captured a pair of ex-Leyton Corporation Class E/3 tramcars – Nos 183 and 166, working Routes 33 and 35 – as they passed; the former entering the Subway and the latter leaving it.

London – Tuesday 23 March 1948

A few moments later, from the same vantage point, No 593, a Class E/1 car of 1930 passed by on driver training. The resumption of London's tramway abandonment programme was still two years off; so new motormen were still needed. Practical tuition on 'the road' followed days of instruction into the mechanical and electrical side of tramcars, plus a short period working alongside experienced motormen. The first Waterloo Bridge's piers were Portland stone and in 1923 two of them began to sink. The bridge was demolished in 1936 amid much controversy and protest, construction of its replacement not being completed until well into World War 2. Most workers on site were women, so it was known locally as 'Ladies' Bridge'. The tramcar was one of a batch of 50, which used the fleet numbers, trucks and electrical equipment from Class F and G single-deck Kingsway Subway cars. They were the most modern vehicles in this the largest class of tramcars in London.

An Olympic Summer

London – Tuesday 23 March 1948

Turning back to the Subway portal, V. C. Jones next caught E/3 Class car No 191, another ex-Leyton Corporation vehicle of 1930, as it swung right towards Westminster, the sun gleaming on its windscreen. Standing back revealed the barrier upon which he had been leaning, the base of which seems to have been made from old Underground sleepers! The rebuilding of Waterloo Bridge required the diversion of the side entrance to the tramway to a new position centrally underneath the bridge; this opened on 21 November 1937. Partially open to traffic in 1942, the new bridge was not formally opened until 10 December 1945. It cost approximately £1m and is London's longest bridge with a span of 1,250 feet. To the far right the original entrance/exit to the subway can be glimpsed.

London – Tuesday 23 March 1948

Moments later Class E/3 car No 1928 of 1930, working route 31, paused at the subway portal awaiting its opportunity to swing onto the Embankment, affording V. C. Jones a chance to record details of the portal. This made great use of concrete, but was faced in part with the Portland stone from which the new Waterloo Bridge, designed by Sir Giles Gilbert Scott, was built. The centre slot of the conduit current-collection system used on much of London's tramways was prone to becoming blocked or clogged by debris, so regular basic cleaning was vital; this task is being carried out by an employee with a broom, pictured left of shot.

London – Saturday 27 March 1948

Following the final abandonment of tramways in London in 1952 the Embankment trackbed was redesignated a carriageway, and remains in this use today. Because of the arrangement that pertained whilst the trams operated, a lengthy waiting shelter had long been provided on a narrow island at Blackfriars, between the roadway and the tramway, to provide a refuge for intending passengers and a safe place for those ending their journeys to disembark. The former LCC Tramways symbol can be seen on the top of the destination notice.

Maidstone – Sunday 28 March 1948

Maidstone's history developed around the River Medway and the surrounding countryside. Paper mills, stone quarrying, brewing and the cloth industry all flourished there. In 1948 the town was on the route of the Olympic Torch Relay from Dover to Wembley, which passed through the following towns: Dover, Canterbury, Charing, Maidstone, Westerham, Redhill, Reigate, Dorking, Guildford, Bagshot, Ascot, Windsor, Slough, and Uxbridge, between 21.00 on Wednesday 28 July 1948 and 16.00 on 29 July. Overseeing the progress of the Olympic torch as it passed through Kent was a Maidstone man, Richard Wells (1914-2004). He was a keen sportsman in his youth and a member of Maidstone Harriers. Wells won the National Junior Championship in the 440-yard event at White City in 1933 and was in line for a place in the British squad for the 1940 Olympics, which never took place because of World War 2. During the war Richard Wells was posted to India, and one of the duties he was assigned to guard the Mahatma Gandhi when the British incarcerated the future Indian prime minister.

Many of the visits to places outside London that V. C. Jones made were as part of tours by the Southern Counties Touring Society (SCTS). One such was to Maidstone on Sunday 28 March 1948. Visits were always transport-related with ample opportunity for photography, and this one included a tour of the town's trolleybus system. Outside the Westminster Bank trolleybus No 69 was photographed awaiting to depart on the Sutton Road/Grove Road. The side advert, for Reg Brett, serves as a reminder of the days before the Betting and Gaming Act, 1960 was enacted, when there were no legal betting shops and 'bookies' runners' acted as intermediaries between punters and turf accountants. Following the Act becoming law, on 1 May 1961, betting shops opened at a rate of 100 a week and after six months there were already 10,000 set up! Otherwise, there doesn't seem much going on – was the Carlton Café open?

Maidstone – Sunday 28 March 1948

Some fellow SCTS members can be glimpsed at left as they toured Tonbridge Road depot. Working the Wheatsheaf route, Corporation trolleybus No 54, a Sunbeam W with Roe H62R body, new in 1943, was parked on the depot apron. It is a very crisp, clean-looking vehicle, and was clearly shot from the vantage point of another bus. All of Maidstone's buses carried adverts for Fremlins Ale & Stout – something that makes photographs of them instantly identifiable.

Fremlins 'Pale Ale Brewery' was in Earl Street. The premises dated back to c1790 and was acquired in the 1860s by the Fremlin family, who operated from there until they were taken over by Whitbread in 1967 – No 54's side advert is therefore very appropriate! Brewing was moved to Flowers in Cheltenham and the Earl Street Brewery closed in 1972. In the 1990s production was moved to Castle Eden but the Fremlin brand was dropped in 1997.

Maidstone – Sunday 28 March 1948

Maidstone Corporation also operated a fleet of buses, of which No 48 was a Guy Arab. It was photographed departing a stand in High Street, behind which SCTS members can be seen walking about. The side advert for the Maidstone & District Laundry Co Ltd serves as a reminder that most towns once had such a service, which would collect laundry – usually bedsheets – launder and deliver them, cleaned and pressed, often in a neat parcel in blue paper tied up with string. The Maidstone laundry was on the road to Loose, a village 2½ miles to the south, which, before it occurs to anyone, did have a Women's Institute!

Watford – Monday 29 March 1948

Business took V. C. Jones to Watford on Monday 29 March 1948, where, outside the railway station (seen at right) he photographed London Transport ST136 working Route 336 (Watford-Chesham). ST136 was one of only six lowbridge STs, with special bodies by Short Bros of Rochester. When introduced in October 1929, the prototype vehicle – ST1 –

was a revolutionary bus for London, having a full-width enclosed rear platform and an enclosed, straight staircase, roller blinds front and rear and the cab even had a windscreen from new! 'Tin tabernacles', like the one seen at left, were once a very common sight. David Rowell & Co of Westminster made many of them and in recent years they have become the focus of much interest.

Watford – Monday 29 March 1948

The upper deck of ST136 showing an unusual feature - twin gangways with 3-in-a-row bench seats. Owing to their special bodywork, these lowbridge STs survived longer in service than any others in their class. The bus had entered service in May 1930, passing to the LPTB (Country Area) in July 1933 and since 1944 had been garaged at Amersham and worked route 336 (Watford-Chesham). In January 1950 it was fitted with a diesel engine and worked route 127 from Merton garage, until withdrawal from service in July 1951; in February 1953 it was sold to W. North of Leeds.

London – Saturday 10 April 1948

Saturday 10 April 1948 saw V. C. Jones in Camberwell garage where he photographed ST722 – one of a class of 1139 similar vehicles introduced from January 1930, which London Transport had inherited from the LGOC. The vehicle had entered service in Leyton in March 1931 and between August 1943 and October 1944 had been converted to operate on producer gas instead of petrol, for which purpose it would have towed a small trailer on which the gas making apparatus was installed. When pictured, ST722 had just been transferred to Camberwell and was receiving a pre-service check and clean. Behind the front wheel a paper sticker can be seen noting that nominal ownership of the bus had transferred from the LPTB to the London Transport Executive (LTE) on 1 January. After moving on to Alperton garage, ST722 was withdrawn from service in January 1950 and sold for scrap to Daniels of Rainham.

PREVIOUS PAGE:
London – Saturday 10 April 1948

At the tramway side of Camberwell depot Snow broom car No 017 was seen with a youthful driver at the controls! This car was allocated to New Cross depot, and had formerly been Class B Car No 153. The LPTB had 21 such converted cars. Part of the snow broom equipment can be glimpsed beneath the front platform. A chain and gear drive, engaged only when the car was in motion, drove a rotary broom which was set at 15° off square and had the effect of sweeping snow forward and to the left of the car as it advanced.

Wimbledon – Sunday 11 April 1948

At the start of what would prove to be a busy Sunday, V. C. Jones began in Wimbledon. At the tram terminus by the Town Hall he caught a pair of Class E/1 cars: No 1611 of 1911/2 and No 1844 of 1922. Both retained their LCC Tramways perforated 'Venner' route number stencils, which were illuminated from behind at night. Although outwardly most of London's trams looked similar, there were many detailed differences. For instance, No 1611 – the older car – had a lower dash panel, requiring the gap between this and the standard vestibule screen to be filled with leather, which was flexible enough to cope with the movement between the two. In the meantime, the driver and conductor of Car No 1844 chat whilst keeping a wary eye on the photographer.

Peckham – Sunday 11 April 1948

The Greenwich works of G. A. Harvey and Co (London) Ltd generated quite a number of abnormal loads, such as this fractionating column, *en route* to America, photographed in Peckham Rye on Sunday 11 April 1948. It is seen passing the front of Jones & Higgins in Rye Lane – Peckham's most prestigious shop. Established at 3 Rye Lane in 1867, the firm had expanded in the later years of the 19th century. The store survived the Blitz but sadly not the change in shopping habits. It was taken over by John Lewis in 1940, sold on in 1948 and had its name changed to the Houndsditch in the mid-1970s, but closed down in 1981. The site was later cleared to make way for the Aylesham Shopping Centre.

Peckham – Sunday 11 April 1948

Jones & Higgins was a locally iconic department store and grew into a popular and fashionable place to shop up until its eventual closure in 1981. The Jones & Higgins buildings covered one side of the street at the bottom end of Rye Lane and often attracted many famous faces (notably Diana Dors) to open up sales events and turn on Christmas lights. Here the abnormal load had to make a sharp left turn, enabling V. C. Jones to take this shot showing the column's dimensions clearly. Lots of other photographers were on hand to record the scene. The one in the centre foreground has a press camera with an open frame viewfinder on top.

Peckham – Sunday 11 April 1948

Having negotiated the turn successfully, some of the hauliers' crew return to the cab. Behind the column is the 'Kentish Drovers', an old-established tavern in the Peckham Road, which is said to have existed here for about two centuries. When Peckham was a village, surrounded by green fields, the 'Kentish Drovers' was a well-known halting-place for cattle-dealers, etc., on the road to Kent. The policeman superintending the operation seemed to be enjoying himself enormously.

Peckham – Sunday 11 April 1948

Everyone's attention seems to have been caught by the slow progress of the fractionating column, including that of the conductor and passengers on Class E/1 car 1406, which was working duty 13 of route 40 that day. Edward Box & Co Ltd's Scammell tractor No 187 was limited to a speed of 12mph! It's remarkable that, even on a Sunday, most of the children are in their school uniform, or something very close to it. The whole experience of following such a heavy load on its slow progress must have been a great adventure then.

Peckham – Sunday 11 April 1948

Edward Box's crew spent most of their time running or walking alongside the tractor and its large trailer load as demonstrated in this view. They were needed as, on many occasions, branches, road signs and other impediments to their progress had to be 'persuaded' back to clear the passage of the load. The array of chimney pots on the houses behind is very impressive – each grate had a flue and each flue had a separate pot.

Peckham – Sunday 11 April 1948

Boys closely followed the column's slow progress on bikes or on foot. The lamp standard to the right bears a notice for a local road safety scheme, exhorting pedestrians to 'Halt at the Kerb - and Look!' This had been running in various parts of London for about a year.

Peckham – Sunday 11 April 1948

The column's unofficial escort can be seen easily keeping pace with its slow progress as a mercifully straight piece of road opens up ahead. Here at least the tractor could approach something close to its 12mph maximum speed. The trailer bogie wheels had solid tyres, which could easily damage kerbs if the load had to cross them whilst negotiating a bend. In such instances large metal discs would be laid down to protect them.

London – Sunday 11 April 1948

These scenes are reminiscent of the 1952 British Transport Films production *Dodging The Column*, which documented the movement of a 137-foot-long distillation column, 500 miles by road from Harveys of Greenwich to Grangemouth in Scotland. Here motorcycle outriders and a tram are visible in the gap between the column and Feltham No 2157, whilst police cars and unofficial escorts follow on behind. Originally London United Tramways No 388, the car was withdrawn from service in September 1951, and went on to see further service in Leeds.

London – Sunday 11 April 1948

Occupying the full width of the roadway, the fractionating column inches across Lambeth Bridge accompanied by police motorcycle outriders with a police car behind. The bridge had been opened on 19 July 1932 by King George V and was well used to this kind of 'abuse' as it was the preferred route for abnormal loads. There are three Edward Box & Co staff in the cab although one at least looks about ready to jump out again.

London – Sunday 11 April 1948

V. C. Jones followed the fractionating column for some distance after it crossed Lambeth Bridge. In his final shot of the occasion, taken in Grosvenor Gardens, Victoria, the details of the load are once again clear. The column weighed 108 tons and had a safe working pressure of 480 lbs/sq in.

Its recipient – the Lummus Co of New York – had been established in 1907 and earlier in 1948 had reopened its London office, which had closed during the war. The company still exists.

London – Saturday 17 April 1948

The Birmingham & Midland Motor Omnibus Co Ltd branded the side of their buses with the plainer 'Midland' and, because their livery was bright red, they became known as 'Midland Red'. Midland No 2061 was 11 years old, on a private charter and clearly well away from home when V. C. Jones photographed it in The Strand. Note that the roof vents are all open, as most of the passengers are smoking. Each of them, additionally, is wearing a hat.

London – Saturday 17 April 1948

It must have been a good day for private charters, as the next such bus V. C. Jones encountered was centre-entrance Lansdowne AEC Regent No 38, at Chelsea. The company took its name from the road in Leytonstone in which its offices were located. Lansdowne was really a bus dealer by trade and bought old vehicles from Maidstone & District, Northern General, Midland Red, East Kent, etc but also operated a few buses and coaches of its own, mainly for school runs. Some aspects of these vehicles seem to have etched indelible memories on some people, who recall them as being either 'in a very sorry state' or as great places to play when parked up between journeys.

London – Friday 23 April 1948

On a Friday evening V. C. Jones photographed London Transport Leyland Cub C106 in Westminster on route 53A. This was the first of eight vehicles normally dedicated to London Transport's Inter-Station service operated on behalf of the main-line railway companies, which continued following Nationalisation of the railways on 1 January 1948. By this time the service was an evening-only one. Unusually, their livery was blue and cream. The raised rear section made room for the stowage of luggage beneath. Note the old taxicab to the far left.

London – Friday 23 April 1948

On the same evening V. C. Jones captured Leyland Cub CR32 in Kingsway working route 68 to West Norwood. The CR-class vehicles were introduced from 1939. They had rear engines, pneumatically-operated front entrance doors and seated only 20. Withdrawn during the war, they were reintroduced to serve as relief buses in Central London in 1946.

London – Friday 23 April 1948

Continuing his peregrinations V. C. Jones came across a Bedford OB coach operated by Cronshaw's. The OB model was introduced in 1939, but only 73 were built before production ceased for the Second World War. It reappeared in an unchanged form at the end of the war continuing in production until 1950. Some 12,766 OBs were produced. Memories of Cronshaw's coaches are mixed: they took children on outings, but they had also been used to evacuate others on the outbreak of war.

London – Saturday 24 April 1948

It was Cup Final Day in London and ST856, one of 191 AEC Regents inherited by London Transport from Thomas Tilling Ltd, is working route 53A through Westminster. Having entered service in July 1930, ST856 had been loaned to Stockton Corporation between January 1942 and May 1944, and when photographed had just returned to service in London working route 11 out of Hammersmith garage. By 1948 only 69 of the 191 Tilling STs remained in service, and they were also used for driver training, as staff canteens and to bolster services on such occasions as the Cup Final. Here supporters, with their tasselled hats, scarves and rosettes, are making their way down the open rear stairs. Manchester United and Blackpool contested the 1948 FA Cup Final at Wembley Stadium. United, who hadn't appeared in an FA Cup Final in 39 years, won 4-2, with two goals from Jack Rowley and one apiece from Stan Pearson and John Anderson. Eddie Shimwell and Stan Mortensen scored Blackpool's goals. With his goal, Shimwell became the first fullback to score at Wembley. ST856's fate was less auspicious; it was withdrawn from Uxbridge Garage in January 1949 and scrapped.

London – Sunday 25 April 1948

'Felthams' were clearly much in evidence in 1948. V. C. Jones photographed No 2080 (ex-MET No 336) in Southcroft Road, Tooting on 25 April 1948 passing Gosdens newsagents and tobacconists. The shop is festooned with advertisements, including one (partly obscured by the tram) for Lilliput, a literary and arts magazine published between July 1937 and July 1960, which featured the works of John Betjeman, Robert Graves, Julian Huxley, Walter de la Mare and Stephen Spender, amongst others. 'Feltham' No 2080 was withdrawn in October 1950 and subsequently saw further service in Leeds.

London – Saturday 8 May 1948

Low spring sunshine was casting long shadows and highlighting the gleaming bodywork and gold lining on E/1r No 1391 when V. C. Jones photographed it following another car off Westminster Bridge at the County Hall end on 8 May 1948. Built in 1910, No 1391 was withdrawn in January 1952 and scrapped at Penhall Road. From this point trams could either proceed straight on along Westminster Bridge Road or swing right along Lambeth Palace Road, past St Thomas Hospital, seen at right.

London – Sunday 9 May 1948

Many photographs of London trams were taken on enthusiasts' specials, such as the SCTS tour V. C. Jones documented on Sunday 9 May 1948. One of the cars allocated was HR/2 No 1885. In this selection she is first seen ascending the entrance ramp from the Kingsway Subway in Southampton Row. Car No 1885 was one of just four HR/2s to be included in the tramcar rehabilitation programme, and was refurbished in November 1936. She was withdrawn in May 1952 and broken up at Penhall Road.

London – Sunday 9 May 1948

A short distance from Southampton Row, just off camera to the left,
V. C. Jones captured No 1885 working through Bloomsbury. No other
photograph from this series makes the point that this was a Sunday better
than this one – during the week the streets would have been thronging
with traffic. The car's headlight is still on from when it was passing through
the subway.

London – Sunday 9 May 1948

For part of this particular tour, No 1885 was following the 33 route, and is seen at its Manor House terminus at the far end of Finsbury Park; the enthusiasts are disembarking to stretch their legs and photograph the tram. In the shopping parade behind is 'The Manor' greengrocery; the builders Patman & Fotheringham are refurbishing the flats above. Ten years later, this firm became embroiled in a legal action concerning insurance policies taken out on building contracts, leading to a major revision in the law.

London – Sunday 9 May 1948

From Manor House the SCTS special returned through the Kingsway Subway and headed for Wimbledon. Here No 1885 is posed in Tooting High Street, by the junction with Longley Road. There was a change pit here, where Wimbledon-bound cars changed from the conduit to the overhead wire, as No 1885 has just done. The boy on the driver's platform is cradling his own camera and seems at ease, unlike the glum-looking boy in the second window! The man standing behind the car was one of the most enthusiastic when it came to disembarking from the tramcar each time it stopped – as will be seen below.

London – Sunday 9 May 1948

No 1885 is seen at the terminus of routes 2 and 4 outside Wimbledon town hall, in the company of class E/1 1802. The stand here was in the middle of the road, with only some subterranean public toilets for company. It was also a trolleybus turning circle, the wires from which can be seen curving around the tramcars. The scene is alive with interest. To the right is the Wimbledon branch of Kennards, a department store whose main branch was in nearby Croydon. Kennards were famous for their innovative sales ploys and in December 1936 they held demonstrations of television sets – amongst the first seen anywhere. Beyond is Mitchell & Scott, the tailors, whose shop boasted a pair of neon scissors, which repeatedly opened and closed. Good initials too – would make a good brand name!

London – Sunday 9 May 1948

On the return run from Wimbledon, No 1885 resumed the conduit at Longley Road change pit. To the far right much of the change-pit paraphernalia can be seen. The boy on the driver's platform peers around curiously awaiting the off and the insertion of the plough whilst the pointsman awaits his signal. The tramcar's windows reveal reflections of Wimbledon-bound car No 1849 and an original enamel stop sign. Ahead and left of the car are Carlwell Street and Aldis Street as Tooting High Street continues to Tooting Broadway.

London – Sunday 9 May 1948

Plough inserted, No 1885 has pulled forward but waits while SCTS members – led by its most eager enthusiast – disembark to photograph the scene. The conductor secures the trolley rope and exchanges pleasantries with the pointsman. Meanwhile, the driver of Class E/1 car No 1849 of 1922 – who looks like he is wearing sunglasses – awaits the pointsman's services. From here No 1885 worked back through to Croydon and on to the terminus of Route 42 in Thornton Heath. Note the RESERVED details on the windscreen immediately above the conductor's hat! All vehicles chartered by the SCTS displayed these.

An Olympic Summer

London – Sunday 9 May 1948
On the return run through Croydon, V. C. Jones caught this wonderfully framed driver's eye view from the front platform of No 1885. To the right is a branch of Barclays Bank and a pair of cyclists, to the left ex-Walthamstow car No 2045 of 1927 working route 8. This car also had a low dash, which had to be breached with leather!

London – Sunday 9 May 1948
At Thornton Heath Pond No 1885 was caught with an unidentified Class E/3 car. This was the junction for the Thornton Heath branch. Borwick's Baking Powder was made by George Borwick & Sons, whose other staple product was custard powder. On just these products great wealth was made and in 1916 Sir Robert Borwick, the founder's son, was created the 1st Baron Borwick of Hawkshead.

London – Sunday 9 May 1948

Next No 1885 ran past Purley depot, pausing so that those aboard could glimpse some of the run-down cars stored there. To the right is ex-West Ham Corporation car No 328, which was one of a small batch of six cars dating from 1925. It was not fitted with a vestibule screen. This car worked route 65 – the last to operate in North London – until it was withdrawn on 9 June 1940. No 328 did not work in service again, being stored first at Hampstead depot and then at Purley before being scrapped in 1949. To the left is Class E/1 car No 1732 of 1922, which was formally withdrawn from service and scrapped at Brixton Hill depot in May 1949.

London – Sunday 9 May 1948

Panning left, V. C. Jones also caught Class E/1 car No 1754 of 1922, which was also scrapped at Brixton Hill Depot in May 1949. Purley depot looked little better than the cars stored there. In fact it had ceased to be an operating depot in 1937 and thereafter was used to store and break up cars withdrawn from service. With the closure of the nearby Thornton Heath Depot in 1949 for rebuilding as a bus garage, Purley was reopened as a running shed – hence why these long-stored cars were taken to Brixton for breaking up.

Romford – Saturday 15 May 1948

The City Motor Omnibus Co Ltd had been operating services between Kentish Town in London and Southend since 1928. In 1936 they acquired a number of operators in the Brentwood area and in 1938 a re-styled City Coach Company built a new Head Office there. Perhaps the most famous of their vehicles were prewar six-wheel single-decker Leyland LT class Tigers, one of which is seen here.

Romford – Saturday 15 May 1948

In Romford later the same day, V. C. Jones spied this Westcliff-on-Sea Guy Arab double-decker in Park End Road, Romford working Route 2A to Vange via Laindon – both villages near Basildon. The bus side carries an advert for 'Genasprin – The SAFE form of Aspirin – Sees You Through'.

Genasprin was introduced in 1919 by Genatosan Ltd, the British makers of Sanatogen, to counter fears that many of the medicinal products in use in the country at that time were in fact produced in German chemical laboratories – hence the use of the word 'safe', maybe?

Brentwood – Saturday 15 May 1948

The driver and conductor of City Coach Leyland Tiger LS8 pose with their charge in the spring sunshine of a May Saturday morning in Brentwood before departing for Wood Green.
The section of City Coach's route beyond Wood Green to Kentish Town had been abandoned on 1 October 1947 and Brentwood became the centre of their operations. To the rear and right of the coach is another single-decker, alongside with a regimented group of schoolgirls is walking – a reminder that it was not uncommon for children to go to school on Saturday mornings too!

Brentwood – Saturday 15 May 1948

With an overflowing bus stop opposite, City Coach Leyland Lion LT8 pulls away from its stop in Brentwood, displaying Wood Green. City Coach was acquired by Westcliff-on-Sea Motor Services Ltd in 1952, which was itself absorbed by Eastern National in 1955. Gone was City's guarantee to get you home provided that you were in the queue before departure time – no matter how many vehicles they had to call up! None of this yet troubled the eager group waiting opposite, with their cases and hampers, all looking forward to a good day out!

Gidea Park – Saturday 15 May 1948

Gidea Park is part of Romford, on the northeast edge of Greater London. It was the location for the Romford Garden Suburb, which was constructed in 1910/11 as an exhibition of town planning. More than 100 architects designed small cottages and houses and a competition was held to select the best town-planning scheme for the suburb. The bus is a Leyland PD1/1 with a Beadle L52R body, which was new to City Coach in 1946, passing first to Westcliff Motor Services and then to Eastern National – it was also later converted to an open-top configuration. Behind the City Coach double-decker is a yard selling second-hand vehicles, and the advert behind it for Ediswan Starter Batteries is a reminder of the days in which cars had separate batteries for starting and lighting..

Gidea Park – Saturday 15 May 1948

At Gidea Park V. C. Jones also photographed six-wheel London Transport AEC Renown LT1375, which was showing wartime-restricted blinds for route 87 (Rainham War Memorial-Barking-Romford-Gidea Park). Introduced in July 1932, the bus had a diesel engine from new. It was displaced from service the following year by the arrival in large numbers of RT-family buses.

The bus-side poster is for Gentleman's Agreement, which had won the Best Picture, Best Director (for Elia Kazan) and Best Actress in a Supporting Role (for Celeste Holm) Academy Awards in 1947.

Guildford – Monday 17 May 1948

In addition to other wartime privations, Guildford was also in range of the V1 flying bombs launched against southeast England in the summer of 1944. Five landed in the town, but most fell on the outskirts. On 28 June 1944 a V1 exploded in the middle of Stoke Recreation Ground. If it had fallen even a short distance on either side it would have killed many people living in the busy streets around. The post-war years were difficult for many in Guildford, with an acute shortage of homes. Some families even took to squatting in larger empty houses in the area, as well as in former army huts. In 1948 the Olympic Torch Relay from Dover was scheduled to pass through Guildford on its way to Wembley, approaching from the Dorking direction. At Guildford a civic welcome had been arranged and every available policeman was needed to control the early morning crowds that lined the route.

Monday 17 May 1948 was the Spring Bank Holiday and V. C. Jones appears to have gone to Guildford. There he found Aldershot & District's D583, a Dennis Falcon with a 20-seat body by Strachan's, which was new in 1939. The bus is bound for Horsell, a village on the outskirts of Woking, one of whose claims to fame is that early in H. G. Wells' 'The War of the Worlds' the narrator observes a meteor landing on Horsell Common!

Guildford – Monday 17 May 1948

V. C. Jones may only have been in Guildford between trains, as he seems to have spent most of his time close to the railway station. There he photographed Aldershot & District Guy Arab II G26, which was delivered to the company new in 1945. It is bound for Onslow Village, which was developed by the Onslow Village Association to provide decent working-class housing following World War 1. They acquired 646 acres of land from the 5th Earl of Onslow in 1920 and by March 1922 had erected 91 houses, the village eventually comprising some 600 homes.

Guildford – Monday 17 May 1948

Next to the stop was Aldershot & District D364, a 1934 Dennis Lancet with a 30-seat body by Strachans. It is showing Guildford Park Street, which is in the town centre. V. C. Jones was lucky to catch this bus – it was withdrawn later in 1948 after an eventful career, which included use as an ambulance between September 1939 and 1945. The Bank Holiday crowds were certainly gathering.

Guildford – Monday 17 May 1948

Rounding the corner to the station next was Aldershot & District D492, a Dennis Lance 2 which was new in 1937. It was originally fitted with a Strachan body, but was re-bodied by East Lancs in 1944, at the same time being fitted with a Gardner 5LW diesel engine. The vehicle gave 21 years' service, being withdrawn in 1958.

Guildford – Monday 17 May 1948

Back outside the station, V. C. Jones found this Safeguard Dennis single-decker showing Dennisville. The latter was the product of some social engineering by the bus manufacturer in 1933 when they built a large estate of 102 workers' houses on what was then the outskirts of Guildford. These were to house workers from Coventry, Dennis having bought White & Poppe, the noted engine manufacturers there. Today Dennisville survives in name only.

Guildford – Monday 17 May 1948

Frank Hutchins and Sydney Hayter founded the Yellow Bus Service in 1928, when they started a route from Guildford to Camberley via Wood Street and Normandy. This displeased the Aldershot & District Traction Co, which tried to obtain a licence for a closely competing route in November 1928. Nonetheless, the underdog survived and fended off Aldershot & District until Yellow surrendered the route in the face of falling business in 1954. Here a Yellow Bus Service Bedford OB waits outside the offices of the West Surrey Farmers Association.

Guildford – Monday 17 May 1948

Another operator working into Guildford was Tillingbourne Valley Services Ltd. Here their single-decker No 6 waits beside busy stops next to a wall of posters, which give a glimpse of cultural life in Guildford in May 1948. Advance notice was given of the Co-operative Day celebration in Stoke Park on Saturday 3 July. At the cinema from Monday 17 May for six days were: In Which We Serve (1942), Lady Hamilton (aka That Hamilton Woman) (1941) and My Gal Sal (1942) – none of which were exactly 'current' releases! The Theatre Royal, Aldershot, offered Ben Travers' Rookery Nook whilst the Guildford Theatre had Arnold Ridley's The Ghost Train.

Guildford – Monday 17 May 1948

A run out into the country on a B. Hammond & Sons single-decker brought V. C. Jones to Wonersh, with its unique multi-purpose road sign/waiting shelter and traffic island. The men talking are outside The Grantley Arms, which dates back to the early 17th century. Under the circumstances, the ladies remaining on the bus would have had a while longer to wait.

Hastings – Sunday 23 May 1948

Hastings had a special connection to the Olympic games. It was the home of the Olympic historian Ian Buchanan (1932-2008). He ran the half-mile in the English Schools for Sussex twice while at Hastings Grammar School and attended the 1948 Olympics, where his love of athletics and the Olympics blossomed. He became close friends with Ross and Norris McWhirter, the twin brothers who founded The Guinness Book of Records. He also joined the London Athletics Club and helped the McWhirters with athletics statistics. In 1991 Ian Buchanan sponsored a group of Olympic historians to meet at The Duke of Clarence pub in Hammersmith and there the International Society of Olympic Historians (ISOH) was formed. His best contribution to the history of Britain at the Olympics is the definitive work, British Olympians, published by Guinness in 1991. In 1997 he was presented with the Olympic Order in Silver by the IOC president, Juan Antonio Samaranch.

The SCTS visited Hastings on Sunday 23 May 1948. In 1935 Maidstone & District Motor Services Ltd purchased the Hastings Tramways Company, which brought trolleybuses into its fleet. Although the vehicles were repainted into the company's green and cream livery, the 'Hastings Tramway' name was retained until 1957. Here SCTS and company officials pose against an unidentified trolleybus.

THIS PAGE
Hastings – Sunday 23 May 1948

Hastings boasts two funicular railways, of which the West Hill one is the older. It comprises two parallel tracks running on a 1:2.9 gradient, and rising 170ft. Some 402ft of the track's total length of 500ft is enclosed within an 18ft x 19ft cylindrical tunnel, constructed from 1.75 million bricks. The West Hill Railway was opened on 25 March 1891 and was bought by Hastings Borough Council in 1947. Following a complete refurbishment in 1991, the railway continues to operate. The passenger cars are of a box-type construction, mounted on a triangular frame, and were supplied by the Midland Railway Carriage & Wagon Company. Each could carry 16 people, 12 seated and four standing. A Crossley gas engine was first used to power the winding gear for the carriages, being replaced by a Tangye diesel engine in 1924 and an electric motor in 1971. V. C. Jones photographed one of the cars from the other one as fellow SCTS members peered back at him.

OVERLEAF
Hastings – Sunday 23 May 1948

Hastings Tramways trolleybus No 42 was one of a batch of 15 Sunbeam W vehicles with Weymann H56R bodies delivered in 1947, so it is little wonder that the SCTS chose it for their tour of the Hastings system. The familiar RESERVED notice is in its usual place on the front windscreen. Hopefully it was warm on board, because, judging by the lady holding her hat on at right, it was a windy day! The trolleybus passed to Maidstone & District and was sold to the Corporation in 1959 when the Hastings system closed.!

Epsom Races – Saturday 5 June 1948

The Epsom Derby, also known as 'The Derby', dates from 1780. Named after Edward Stanley, the 12th Earl of Derby, it is run on the first Saturday in June. Traditionally held at Epsom Downs, in Surrey, over a course of around 2,400m (about 1 mile 4 furlongs), the race was run at Newmarket between 1915 and 1918 and between 1940 and 1945. The field is limited to three-year-old colts and fillies.

Saturday 5 June 1948 was Derby Day at Epsom and V. C. Jones was there to record the scene and the transport used to get the crowds of eager race goers to and from the course. London Transport set up a temporary bus station and visitors were corralled down a rather flimsy-looking alleyway formed from scaffolding poles. They were also all exiting by the entrance!

Epsom Races – Saturday 5 June 1948

The temporary bus station was alongside one of the main car and caravan parks at Epsom. London Transport operated a shuttle service between the racecourse and Morden station. Two ladies look on as CR44 waits to pull away. By 1948 the 20-seater CR class were used as relief vehicles in Central London and were also pressed into service on special occasions – such as Race Days at Epsom.

Epsom Races – Saturday 5 June 1948

London Transport also pressed members of its ageing fleet of STs into service on the Morden Station-Epsom racecourse shuttle service. ST244 had an AEC Regent chassis and a London General Omnibus Co body. It had entered service with the LGOC in July 1930 and been fitted with a spare body following air-raid damage in November 1940. In December 1942 it had been loaned to Midland Red, but returned to London in August 1944, working out of Willesden garage. It would see one more Derby before being withdrawn in October 1949 and sold for scrap to Daniels of Rainham. The chalked cross on the mudguard signifies damage for repair.

An Olympic Summer

Epsom Races – Saturday 5 June 1948

Another CR pressed into service on Derby Day was CR13. New in November 1939, it had been withdrawn into war storage in December 1942 and only reinstated to service in 1946. How well had the departing racegoers seen at right fared? Anyone betting on My Love at 100/9 would have been well pleased – it won! The Aga Khan's horse, ridden by W. Johnstone, beat the rest of the 32-strong field that day.

Southend-on-Sea – Sunday 6 June 1948

Southend-on-Sea and neighbouring Westcliff-on-Sea were on the edge of the reception area for television signals of the Olympic games in 1948. Six years later, the cycle maker, Bates of London, relocated to a new works and shop at 479 London Road, Westcliff-on-Sea. Stan Butler, a former master frame builder with Bates, had built the cycle frames for the 1948 British Olympic cycling team. A late spring visit to Southend on Sunday 6 June 1948 proved fruitful for V. C. Jones. He saw this Westcliff-on-Sea Motor Services' Bristol JO5G, with a 35-seat Eastern Counties body, on Eastern Esplanade, Thorpe Bay, about to depart on route 19A to Leigh (Elm Hotel). The bus was new to its operator in 1937 and like the rest of the fleet passed to Eastern

National in 1955, gaining the fleet number 243 and lasting until around 1958/9. To the left is a helter-skelter – part of Southend's famous Kursaal amusement park. This began as Marine Park; developed by the Tollhurst brothers and opened in 1894. Rides and sideshows were added gradually, and for a time it was known as Luna Park – a common name for amusement parks, derived from the fact that they were open at night. Behind can be glimpsed the frame from one of the gasholders in Southend's gasworks and the background is replete with detail of the lost innocence of British seaside towns – especially the covered helter-skelter!

Southend-on-Sea – Sunday 6 June 1948

Almost 41 years of tramway operation ended in Southend-on-Sea on 8th April 1942 with the closure of the route to Leigh-on-Sea. Services were taken over either by motorbuses or trolleybuses. Here No 133, a Sunbeam W, which was new in 1945/6, is seen negotiating a corner past a branch of the National Bank, *en route* to Hamstel Road, with another trolleybus in hot pursuit. The National Bank merged with the Westminster Bank in 1970 to form the now familiar NatWest.

Southend-on-Sea – Sunday 6 June 1948

Another bus operator working into Southend-on-Sea was Benfleet & District, one of whose Daimler double-deckers is seen arriving in the town having travelled via the splendidly-named Tarpots, Thundersley, Hadleigh and Elms, whilst a Corporation trolleybus pauses at a stop, far left.

Southend-on-Sea – Sunday 6 June 1948

Southend-on-Sea Corporation had been a trolleybus operator since 18 December 1928, when the Prittlewell
tram route – which had been used for trials of trolleybuses in 1925 and 1926 – was converted to this mode
of operation. At that time the trolleybus fleet comprised just two 'rail-less' vehicles. No 115 was one of a batch
of ten AEC 661T/663T vehicles with English Electric bodies acquired in 1932/3. It was showing Priory Park
when photographed, with the original branch of Dixons in the background. The electronic and electrical retailer –
latterly re-branded Currys Digital – was founded as a photographic business in Southend in 1937.

Southend-on-Sea – Sunday 6 June 1948

Southend-on-Sea Corporation had an uneasy relationship with Westcliff-on-Sea Motor Services, but in the mid-1940s an agreement was reached which provided for a limited amount of co-ordination of services. V. C. Jones shot this Westcliff Bristol K/ECW double-decker at a stop working route 7 to Rayleigh High Street. The street detail is excellent, especially the shop blind over Eva Gowns to the right!

Southampton – Sunday 13 June 1948

Southampton suffered 57 air raids during World War 2, by far the worst of which were on 23 and 30 November and 1 December 1940 – events generally referred to as Southampton's Blitz. Over 600 civilians died in the city in air raids during the War and over 900 buildings were destroyed. In 1948 signs of this devastation were still evident.

On 15 May 1948, less than a month before the SCTS toured Southampton aboard car No 108, the corporation had effected the first post-war tramway closure, of the Portswood-Docks route. Car 108 is seen showing 'Special' on route 6A at Southampton Common Permanent Way Depot. Like a lot of the tramcars, No 108 carried bumper sticker for 'Saints vs Birmingham'; however, this was not football but Speedway. The match in question was in the National Trophy at Southampton 'Saints' Bannister Court Stadium on 15 June – sadly the Saints lost 66-41 to Birmingham!

Southampton – Sunday 13 June 1948

At Southampton Common, V. C. Jones photographed one of Southampton Corporation Transport's compulsory tram stop signs.

Southampton – Sunday 13 June 1948

Car 102 showing Royal Pier on route 1 in The Avenue at Southampton Common – note the same 'Saints vs Birmingham' bumper sticker! The car dated from 1924 and remained in service until the end of tramway operation in Southampton in 1949. Tram services along The Avenue ended on 5 March 1949.

Southampton – Sunday 13 June 1948

This Thornycroft SG/NR6 single-decker with a body by Longwell Green belonged to the Bristol Co-Operative Society and was named the 'Queen of the Road'. It is seen in the vicinity of the New Docks, a extensive 7,000ft quay opened in 1934 and built by the Southern Railway.

Southampton – Sunday 13 June 1948

Southampton was the arrival point for some national teams competing in the Olympics, notably the competitors from New Zealand. Each port was assigned a Reception Committee to take charge of disembarking. The Games Organising Committee also employed people to await arrival of ships at ports and assist with confirming the numbers of men and women in each party, and the weight and number of each piece of their baggage.

Docked in Southampton Water on 13 June 1948 was the Durban Castle. Built in Belfast in 1938 to serve on Union Castle's mail run to South Africa, she was converted to an infantry landing ship at the outbreak of World War 2, carrying troops during the invasions of North Africa, Italy and France. She later resumed her role as a mail ship and had hit the headlines in 1947 when cabin steward James Camb murdered actress Gay Gibson on a voyage between Cape Town and Southampton. The Durban Castle was sold for scrap in 1962.

Southampton – Sunday 13 June 1948
From Southampton V. C. Jones ventured to Hythe on board Hants & Dorset Bristol single-decker TS703. It had a Bristol L5G chassis and a Beadle 34-seater body. The following year the bus was rebodied and could then seat 35. She was withdrawn from service in 1957.

Southampton – Sunday 13 June 1948

The reason for going to Hythe was to ride the Pier Tramway, seen here on its way to Hythe. Opened on 1 January 1881, the 2,100ft long pier was built for ferry services to Southampton – the ferry dock can be seen to the left. A baggage line was added in 1909 in response to growing passenger numbers. After the cessation of hostilities in 1918 this was adapted to carry passengers. A new 2ft (60cm) gauge tramway opened in July 1922.

Southampton – Sunday 13 June 1948

The scene at the Hythe end of the pier: the same Brush locomotives still operate to and from the pier-head to this day. The pier-head timber deck was replaced in 1982 and from then until 1986 some £290,000 was spent on considerable repairs to the substructure. On 1 November 2003 Hythe Pier was badly damaged by a dredger, which caused a 150ft breach in the centre of its neck. The end of 2003 saw repairs completed and Hythe Pier re-opened on 7 January 2004, with normal ferry services to Southampton resuming the same day.

Southampton – Sunday 13 June 1948

Back at Southampton Water V. C. Jones found the *Empire Trooper* in dock. She began life as the *Cap Norte*, the second of two sisters built for the Hamburg-South America Line's Europe-South America run after World War 1 and was launched in Hamburg on 8 May 1922. When World War 2 broke out she was stranded in Brazil and, in attempting to return to Germany, on 9 October 1939 she was intercepted off Iceland by HMS *Belfast* and became a British prize.

By June 1940 she had been converted to a troopship at Newcastle and after the war she underwent a major reconstruction at Falmouth, raising her gross tonnage and her accommodation. HMT *Empire Trooper* continued in peacetime service until being retired in April 1955, being scrapped that June.

Southampton – Sunday 13 June 1948

Also in Southampton Water was the RMS *Capetown Castle*. She was launched on 23 September 1937 as a passenger liner. In 1940, she was converted to a troopship, a role she fulfilled until 1946 when she returned to civilian service. The *Capetown Castle* was the first Union Castle Line ship to re-enter service after World War Two, but not without incident. In 1960 a boiler-room explosion killed 7 crewmen and in 1965 20 gold ingots were stolen from her store room. The ship headed off to the breakers' yard in 1967.

Southampton – Sunday 13 June 1948

Southampton was extensively damaged in air raids on 23 and 30 November and 1 December 1940. One of the most badly damaged parts of the city was Above Bar Street, where Corporation car No 103, working Route 1 to Royal Pier, was seen, alongside Manfield & Sons, the shoemakers, at No 124. The tall bomb-damaged building behind is James Woodhouse & Sons, home furnishers. Postwar reconstruction can be seen all around, the shop immediately in front of the tram being refitted on that day and new building continuing behind.

Southampton – Sunday 13 June 1948

A few moments later, Hants & Dorset Leyland PD1 No PD959 working route 47 to Winchester passed by the same location as above, showing more detail of the rebuilding and refitting work then being carried out by William A. Fussell, builders and decorators of 23/24 Orchard Place. The bus remained in service until 1964.

Southampton – Sunday 13 June 1948

Back to the SCTS tour, members relax in the sun at left as Corporation car No 30 on Route 5, showing Floating Bridge, passes by. Part of the second batch of cars, delivered in 1901, this car was built as an open-top double-decker, with a Milnes body on a 4-wheel Brill 21E truck.

Further rebuilding in 1929 produced a top-covered 'Bargate' car with special domed roof. The side advert for Milwards – Southampton's Leading Shoe Service – declares that they were back at their shop in Above Bar, indicating the progress of the ongoing rebuilding work there.

Southampton – Sunday 13 June 1948

A pointsman waves his flag to give the off to the driver of former Southern Railway locomotive No 173 shunting at Town Quay, with a Corporation tram behind. The Southern Railway bought 15 of the American-built locomotives (including one for spare parts) to replace its Class B4 0-4-0T dock shunters based in Southampton. They were fitted with a modified cab and bunker, and under British Railways No 173 was later renumbered 30073.

Southampton – Sunday 13 June 1948
Moments later, viewed from the other side, No 173
pulled away from Town Quay with its load of wagons.

Southampton – Sunday 13 June 1948

During the Olympic games local interest was directed towards the achievements of local rower Richard Burnell. He competed with his rowing partner Bert Bushnell in the Double Sculls event and made it to the final. In that race Burnell and Bushnell competed against Denmark and Uruguay. They went out for the lead from the start, with the Danes second, but Uruguay fought back and overtook the Danes for a time, before the latter regained second place. Despite this going on behind them, Burnell and Bushnell held the lead and won the race in a time of 6min 51.3sec – four clear seconds ahead of the Danes. In the process they won one of the two gold medals gained by the Great Britain team in the whole Games – the other being in the Pairs without Cox event.

At Town Quay a dockyard worker makes his way towards Corporation Car No 100, built by the Tramways undertaking in 1924 on a Peckham P35 truck, whilst others cycle by in the background – possibly it was a shift change. This was the terminus for three routes, including the No 1 to Bassett. The dock building behind the tram is quite imposing, whilst the more modest one to the right was the offices and warehouse of the Itchen Transport Co Ltd, a long-established firm of wharfingers. More recently the area has been regenerated and is now predominantly devoted to tourism and leisure.

Southampton – Sunday 13 June 1948

Ex-Southern Railway Class C14 0-4-0 tank No.3741 was one of two locomotives remaining in capital stock of this small class of ten that were based at Eastleigh for shunting in the Town Quay. Nicknamed the 'Potato Cans', they were 1913 rebuilds of 2-2-0T locomotives originally built in 1892. This one became No 30588 in BR stock and lasted until 1957. The first wagon on the train is ex-LMS.

Southampton – Sunday 13 June 1948

When the last of the Ex-Southern Railway Class C14 0-4-0 tanks were withdrawn in 1960 they owed nobody anything, having proven to be reliable little workhorses. Like most of the other locomotives V. C. Jones photographed six months into railway nationalisation, ex-Southern Railway Class C14 0-4-0 tank No 3741 had not been renumbered or had its previous owner's name removed or obliterated. Here it shunts wagons on Town Quay.

Southampton – Sunday 13 June 1948

V. C. Jones also managed to scout out the other ex-Southern Railway Class C14 0-4-0 tank working on shunting duties at Town Quay – No 30589 – this one had been both rebranded and renumbered! The driver poses patiently in the cab.

Southampton – Sunday 13 June 1948

The Southampton Tramways Co operated a horse tramline along Canute Road to Floating Bridge from early in May 1879. For some reason, possibly the growth in the number of dock railway lines, when the Corporation took over the tramways and electrified them it cut the route back to this point, opposite the Terminus Station. V. C. Jones caught the scene there on 13 June 1948 just as an unidentified Southern Railway 4-6-0 locomotive crossed the road ahead. Note the semaphore signals 'hiding' behind the telegraph and traction poles above the parked cars on the centre left.

Southampton – Sunday 13 June 1948

Back to the SCTS tour, Corporation car No 108 on Route 6A, showing Special, was turned around at Ordnance Curve. The person swinging the pole is possibly one of the SCTS members, given the stance of the Transport Department staff member with his back to the camera. Note the Union flags on the trolley pole rope and the fact that there is no advert on the one side.

To the left are the local offices of the Southampton Rediffusion Service Ltd. Rediffusion was a company formed to distribute radio signals along wired relay circuits, including former tram power lines circuit – a kind of cable radio! In 1947 the British Electric Traction Co purchased a substantial stake in the company.

Southampton – Sunday 13 June 1948

From Ordnance Curve, car No 108 went on to Millbrook where it paused at a compulsory stop revealing that there was an advert on her other side. A solitary SCTS member looks towards our photographer as Corporation staff on the rear platform attempt to chivvy everyone aboard and get on with the tour.

Southampton – Sunday 13 June 1948

At Woolston, V. C. Jones photographed the Itchen Floating Bridge, which crossed the River Itchen between the Chapel area of Southampton on the west bank and the village of Itchen Ferry on the east bank, later known as Woolston. Opened on 23 November 1836, the original wooden ferry was replaced by an iron floating bridge in 1853, and by 1890 a pair of chain ferries ran every fifteen minutes during the daytime. They travelled at a speed of 100 metres a minute (6 kph) and took four minutes to cross the River Itchen. Here Floating Bridge No 10 loads at Woolston.

Southampton – Sunday 13 June 1948

A few minutes later Floating Bridge No 8 arrived from Southampton. In 1972 Southampton City Council decided to build a permanent bridge at the site of the floating bridge, work beginning on 22 March 1974. It was opened on 1 June 1977 and made the Floating Bridge redundant. Accordingly on 11 June 1977 the Itchen Floating Bridge made its final trip.

Southampton – Sunday 13 June 1948

From another paddle steamer, V. C. Jones photographed the RMS *Queen Mary* as she embarked upon yet another transatlantic crossing. The ship had been ordered on 3 April 1929 from John Brown & Co of Clydebank and was launched on 26 September 1934, making her maiden voyage on 27 May 1936. After the war, *Queen Mary* and her younger sister *Queen Elizabeth* dominated the transatlantic passenger trade through the rest of the 1940s and into the 1950s, but in 1958 the first transatlantic jet flight began a new era of competition for the Cunard Queens. On some voyages *Queen Mary* sailed into harbour with more crew than passengers and she was retired from service on 1 December 1967. She is now moored in Long Beach, California as a floating hotel, restaurant and museum.

Gosport Ferry – Sunday 20 June 1948

On Sunday 20 June 1948 V. C. Jones visited Portsmouth. From the order of his negatives he appears to have arrived by bus at Gosport Ferry Terminus, seen here. The scene was a busy one, with Provincial, Hants & Dorset and Premier buses and coaches on stand. Both Palmyra Road and Chantry Road – the destinations of the Premier coach – are in the village of Elson, now a suburb of Gosport, which is older than either Gosport or Portsmouth, being mentioned in a Saxon Charter dated 948 AD.

Portsmouth – Sunday 20 June 1948

Fratton Park in Portsmouth was one of the eleven football grounds where matches were played in the 1948 Olympic football tournament. It was used in the preliminary matches round and it was there that Holland beat Eire by 3 goals to 1, only to go on to lose 4-3 to Great Britain in the First Round at Highbury.

From Gosport, V. C. Jones took the Gosport ferry to Portsmouth where he came upon the aircraft carrier HMS Illustrious. This was the fourth naval vessel to carry the name. She was built by Vickers-Armstrong at Barrow-in-Furness, launched in 1939, and commissioned on 25 May 1940. With a displacement of 23,000 tonnes, she had the capability to carry up to 36 aircraft and was nicknamed 'Lusty' by the men who served on her. On 11 November 1940, she became the first carrier in history to launch a major strike against an enemy fleet in a daring attack against the Italian fleet at Taranto. After the war she was refitted and modernised, but was decommissioned at the end of 1954 and sold, finally being scrapped at Faslane from 3 November 1956.

Portsmouth – Sunday 20 June 1948

Next V. C. Jones photographed the paddle steamer *Whippingham*, which had been built in 1930 by Fairfield Shipbuilding & Engineering at Govan, Glasgow, for year-round service on the Southern Railway's Portsmouth-Ryde railway connection ferry service. For a civilian vessel, PS *Whippingham* had an illustrious (sic) war service; saving 2700 troops on her only crossing during the Dunkirk evacuations; serving as both a minesweeper then as an anti-aircraft vessel; then serving on the South Coast and at the Normandy landings in 1944. After returning to peacetime duties in 1945, the *Whippingham* was withdrawn after the 1962 season and left for ship breakers in Belgium in May 1963.

Portsmouth – Sunday 20 June 1948

V. C. Jones then caught the paddle steamer *Shanklin* embarking for Ryde on the Isle of Wight. She was constructed for the Southern Railway in Southampton in 1924 by John I. Thornycroft and worked the Portsmouth-Ryde Isle of Wight service through to 1949. Two years later she was purchased and reconditioned for excursion work by Cosens and renamed *Monarch*. She operated mainly from Bournemouth to Swanage and had a passenger capacity of 746 and a service speed of 13 knots. After her final season in 1961, she was broken up at Cork.

Portsmouth – Sunday 20 June 1948

Once in Portsmouth, V C Jones rode on the city's trolleybuses. At Cosham he encountered a 'sticks off' situation, catching the conductor of Corporation trolleybus No 280 retrieving the bamboo pole stowed beneath the bus in order to replace the trolley booms. No 280 was an AEC 661T trolleybus, built in 1936-7. Originally it carried the fleet number 80, but was renumbered early in 1938. Beneath the main destination is an advertisement for Timothy Whites (later Timothy Whites & Taylor Ltd); a famous name that once had 600 shops around the UK. They were dispensing chemists who also sold household goods. The business, which was founded in Portsmouth, was taken over by Boots in 1968 and the name disappeared from high streets a few years afterwards. Hovis began life as 'Smith's Patent Germ Bread', but after a nationwide competition it was renamed Hovis - taken from the Latin phrase 'hominis vis' which means 'strength of man'.

An Olympic Summer

Portsmouth – Sunday 20 June 1948

Portsmouth Corporation trolleybus No 240 was caught working route 6 to Dockyard. It was another AEC 661T trolleybus, built in 1936-7 and originally carrying the fleet number 40 before being renumbered in 1938. The driver seems to be making some sort of adjustment. *Everybody's* magazine started life as the *Competitors Weekly* in 1913. By 1928 it was known as *Everybody's Weekly*, but by 1930 it had dropped the 'Weekly' part and was known simply as *Everybody's* – until April 1959 – when it merged with *John Bull* magazine.

Portsmouth – Sunday 20 June 1948

If clocks are to be believed it is 10.42 on Sunday 20 June 1948 and V. C. Jones was in London Road, North End, Portsmouth, looking towards Gladys Avenue. The imposing building centre right was the Booking Office and Garage for Southdown Motor Services. To the right a policeman in a white coat is on point duty directing traffic, whilst the car far right still has its wartime headlight mask fitted.

Portsmouth – Sunday 20 June 1948

Crossing the road, V. C. Jones took this view along London Road, revealing just how precarious a job point duty was! A Southdown double-decker is just pulling past The Clarence Gardens pub at 118 London Road. This prominent pub in North End's shopping district was a Long's house; Long & Co's Southsea Brewery was in Hambrook Street. The company was registered in 1924 but only traded for nine years, being taken over in 1933; brewing ceased in 1934. Two years later architect A. E. Cogswell produced a modern design for The Clarence Gardens and the pub was rebuilt in 1937, being clad in faience. It underwent a major refit in 1995 and in 2005 was given a new name, 'The Mischief'.

Portsmouth – Sunday 20 June 1948

The northern extremity of Portsmouth's trolleybus system was the less-than-romantically-named 'Cosham Compound' which had also served the city's former tramway system. There, V. C. Jones photographed trolleybus No 202 – an AEC 661T trolleybus, built in 1934. Originally it carried the fleet number 2, but was renumbered in 1938. It was one of the first four trolleybuses acquired for the undertaking.

Portsmouth – Sunday 20 June 1948

This view of Portsmouth Corporation trolleybus No 296, working route 14, reveals why Cosham was called a 'compound' – note the piles of sets and other materials piled up in the middle distance! The trolleybus was an

AEC 661T, built in 1936-7. Originally it carried the fleet number 96, but was renumbered in 1938.

Portsmouth – Sunday 20 June 1948

From Cosham V. C. Jones went to Hilsea, where the overhead was very complicated in order to separate vehicles working three routes. The petrol station to the left was very stylish and the fully licensed roadhouse would have been most welcome to passing motorists. No 201 working route 13 to South Parade Pier was an AEC 661T trolleybus, built in 1934. Originally it carried the fleet number 1, but was renumbered in 1938. It was one of the first four trolleybuses

acquired for the undertaking. The bus-side advert is for SO-TAIST-EE extract, which was made by Tyne Brand, a company established in North Shields by Richard Irvin who set up a factory there in 1901 to can herring. 'Tyne Brand' herrings were famous and sold all over the world. During the two world wars the company expanded its range of products to include canned meats and other tinned goods, including pet foods. Spillers bought them in 1967.

Portsmouth – Sunday 20 June 1948

Back at Cosham Compound, V C Jones took three detailed photographs of Portsmouth Corporation trolleybus No 214
(RV 4662) a Sunbeam MS3 vehicle built in 1934 as No 14 but renumbered in 1938. The vehicle carried different
advertisements on each side. Here, on the nearside, was a stark reminder about Oldfield Bros' table waters.

Portsmouth – Sunday 20 June 1948

Next, V. C. Jones took this wonderfully detailed front view of No 214.
The red livery showed off the intricate gold lining very well.

OVERLEAF

Portsmouth – Sunday 20 June 1948

Finally, V. C. Jones took this offside ¾ view of No 214 at Cosham Compound,
with the concentric overhead wires making a wonderful pattern above.
To the right a driver stands in front of a shelter left over from tramway days.
Smith & Vosper was established in 1806 and had a bakery at 30 Green Road
Southsea. It was bombed in 1941 and later the business became part of
Mother's Pride. Twenty years later production was transferred to
Manor Park at Eastleigh.

Portsmouth – Sunday 20 June 1948

The southern extremity of the Portsmouth trolleybus system was South Parade Pier in Southsea where there was a turning circle. V. C. Jones saw No 284 – another AEC 661T trolleybus of 1936-7 – working back northwards to Cosham. Originally it carried the fleet number 84, but was renumbered 284 in 1938. The vehicle seems to have been recently outshopped as it appears to be gleaming and is not carrying any advertising.

Portsmouth – Sunday 20 June 1948

On his return to Gosport, V. C. Jones took another shot of HMS *Illustrious*. She was undergoing a major refit and modernisation, which had begun in January 1948 and would not be completed until that August. Thereafter she resumed her role as a Home Fleet training and trials ship.

Portsmouth – Sunday 20 June 1948

Back at Gosport, V. C. Jones shot Provincial AEC Regent I No 44, which had a Park Royal body and entered service in 1939. It served the company well, being withdrawn in 1963, but, following an accident to sister vehicle No 35 in 1964, its body was fitted to the latter and the 'hybrid' vehicle stayed in service until 1967, when it was bought for preservation. It is still seen at shows to this day. The remains of No 44 were sold for scrap on 23 October 1965.

Stewarts Lane – Saturday 26 June 1948

A late June Saturday found V. C. Jones at Stewarts Lane depot. It had opened in February 1862 as the primary motive power depot of the London Chatham & Dover Railway, providing locomotives for services out of the Victoria terminus nearby. Still resplendent in its Southern livery was air-smoothed 'Battle of Britain' No 21C163 *229 Squadron*, built in May 1947. Late in its existence the Southern Railway had adapted the UIC classification system for its locomotives, where '2' and '1' referred to the number of unpowered leading and trailing axles respectively, and 'C' referred to the number of driving axles – in this case three. However, since '21C' was the prefix already used by the 'Merchant Navy' class, 100 was added to the numbers; all these locomotives therefore carried numbers which started '21C1' followed by the individual two-digit identifier. No 21C163 was renumbered 34063 in January 1949. Withdrawn from Salisbury shed on 15 August 1965, it was stored there until that November, then at Eastleigh works until April 1966. Its final mileage was 736,984. Scrapped in May 1966, it was one of the last engines dealt with by Bird's at Bridgend.

An Olympic Summer

Stewarts Lane – Saturday 26 June 1948

Also on shed that day, glimpsed behind and to the right of 229 Squadron was 'N' class locomotive No 811. Richard Maunsell, Chief Mechanical Engineer of the South Eastern & Chatham Railway, designed the 'N' class of locomotives. The first prototype, No 810, emerged from Ashford Works in July 1917, and No 811, seen here (as 1811), was the first production locomotive. They were the first non-GWR design to incorporate most of Churchward's design features, exemplified by the coned boiler and long travel valves, but the outside valve gear represented an advance on Churchward practice. The locomotive was also still in its SOUTHERN livery as late as June 1948.

Stewarts Lane – Saturday 26 June 1948

William Adams was the Locomotive Superintendent of the London & South Western Railway from 1878. One of his last designs was the B4 class 0-4-0T dock tank, the first batch of which appeared in December 1892. Although their footplates were cramped and they had limited coal supplies, the locomotives were powerful and popular with their crews. Not long after V. C. Jones snapped this example, No 88, at Stewarts Lane, it was renumbered 30088, remaining in service until July 1959.

Brighton – Tuesday 20 July 1948

Volk's Electric Railway celebrated its 125th anniversary in 2008 and is the oldest remaining operating electric railway in the world. Opened on 4 August 1883, the line was originally ¼ mile long and 2ft gauge, but its creator – Magnus Volk – immediately set about extending it, at the same time deciding to widen the gauge to 2ft 8½ in. The new 1,440 yard line opened on 4 April 1884. In 1936 Brighton Corporation decided to build a swimming pool at Black Rock – one end of the line – requiring it to be shortened by a few hundred yards. A new Black Rock station was opened on 7 May 1937 and Magnus Volk took control of Car 10 for a journey from the New Station. It was his last public appearance as he died peacefully at home 13 days later.

Brighton – Tuesday 20 July 1948

Open-top buses have long been a feature of British seaside towns, and Brighton was no exception. Brighton Hove & District No 6291 – photographed on 'Sea Front Service' 17 – was an AEC Regent of 1935, which had been rebodied to an open-top configuration in 1946. Given the number of standing passengers it is likely that the bus had just pulled away from a stop; and judging from their macs, hats and overcoats, it is also likely that it was not a very warm day!

Brighton – Tuesday 20 July 1948

The Goldstone Ground – or 'The Goldstone' as it was known locally – was the home ground of Brighton & Hove Albion FC between 1902 and 1997. It was also another of the eleven football grounds where matches were played in the 1948 Olympic football tournament. It was there that Luxembourg beat Afghanistan 6-0 in the preliminary round, going on to be beaten 6-1 by Yugoslavia in the first round at Craven Cottage. The Great Britain team, which was coached by Matt Busby, beat Holland 4-3 in the first round at Highbury; France won 1-0 in the Second Round, also at Highbury, but were beaten 3-1 by Yugoslavia in the semi-final at Wembley. In the third place (bronze medal) play-off match, Great Britain lost 5-3 to Denmark!

V. C. Jones also sought out Brighton's trolleybuses. The first 44 AEC 661T vehicles with Weymann bodies had been delivered in 1939, but had been stored for the duration of the war at Whitehawk depot. No 29 from that first batch was photographed working Route 46A to Preston Drove at the Aquarium, Old Steine terminus. This was the terminus for most of Brighton's trolleybus routes. The wooden building on the right was a relic from tramway days and was used as a staff rest room and passenger shelter. Brighton's last trolleybus ran on 30 June 1961.

Brighton – Tuesday 20 July 1948

In Brighton, certain excursion and longer-distance bus services had been the province of Southdown Motor Service since 1915. Southdown Leyland Titan 171 is seen in front of the company's offices in Pool Valley, working route 119 to Tunbridge Wells. If the clock is to be believed it was 3.09 pm. Behind is 'Ye Olde Bunn Shoppe' of the 18th century and Rowell's clock factory, which was established in 1826. The arrow points on the end of the bay markings are a novel feature!

London – Wednesday 21 July 1948

William Birch began a cab business in Horseferry Road, Westminster, in 1832 and the family remained in transport thereafter. Birch Bros Ltd. was formed in November 1899 and became bus operators in 1904. In November 1928 they inaugurated a service between Bedford and London. By 1948 their route 203 – London-Welwyn-Hitchin-Bedford-Rushden – operated daily and since 1940 had been worked by double-deckers. Here V. C. Jones caught their Leyland PD1 K183 entering King's Cross bus station as a cab overtakes.

London – Wednesday 21 July 1948

A few minutes later V. C. Jones caught Birch Bros K183 leaving King's Cross bus station at the start of its return journey to Rushden. The bus is heeling over somewhat; the conductor can be seen hanging onto the handrail through the still open side door! The vehicle would be withdrawn in 1965, by which time Birch Bros' revenue had been hit by falling passenger numbers. Its last double-deck vehicle ran in 1967, and in 1968/9 the final two routes (203/203M) passed to United Counties.

Olympics – Saturday 31 July 1948

On Saturday 31 July 1948 V. C. Jones travelled to Wembley to look at the transport arrangements for the Olympic games, which had opened two days earlier. The only obvious sign is the billowing Union Jacks on the buildings at right. He caught London Transport L3-class trolleybus No 1447 on route 662 at the Wembley terminus. Wally Kilmister, who was something of a local hero, ran the sports shop far right, which was at the corner of the road that passed the main entrance to the Empire Stadium – the main Olympic venue. Born in New Zealand, Kilmister came to the UK in 1929 to help to introduce the new sport of Speedway, riding for the Wembley Lions. He opened his sports shop in 1936.

Olympics – Saturday 31 July 1948

Many older classes of buses were pressed into service for the Olympics at Wembley. V. C. Jones caught London Transport ST16 on route 83 at Wembley Stadium. This was more correctly known as the Empire Stadium. It was built in exactly 300 days at a cost of £750,000 for the British Empire Exhibition of 1923. The 127,000-capacity stadium was ready with four days to spare before its first event – the FA Cup Final – on 28 April. Bolton Wanderers beat West Ham United 2-0 before an over-capacity crowd estimated at close on 300,000! The stadium closed in October 2000 and was demolished in 2003 for redevelopment, the new Wembley being ready

for the FA Cup Final on 19 May 2007. The LT staff working the Olympics services wore white summer coats – one so attired can be seen approaching the bus to speak with the driver. The bus had entered service with the LGOC in March 1930 and for thirteen months – between October 1943 and November 1944 – had been converted to operate on producer gas to save petrol. ST16 was withdrawn from service one year on from its Olympic duties, being sold for scrap to Daniels of Rainham.

Olympics – Saturday 31 July 1948

V. C. Jones took this overview of the coach park at the Empire Pool (centre left), Wembley. The pool was built in the space of six months for the 1934 Empire Games and housed two pools and a wave machine. The games ran between 4-11 August 1934. Thereafter it was used as a venue for swimming, skating, boxing, etc., plus music. A duty policeman, wearing white sleeve covers, is chatting to a colleague while over to the right a sea of cars can be seen.

OPPOSITE

Olympics – Saturday 31 July 1948

The 1948 Olympics was the Empire Pool's last use as a swimming venue and for 30 years afterwards it became better known as an ice rink and concert hall. Moving in for a closer look at the vehicles parked there on 31 July 1948, V. C. Jones took this shot of some of the London Transport vehicles parked up there, including, from left to right, Q167, RT274, T16 and LTC4. The Q-class buses were mid-engined, the engine being mounted on the offside, behind the front wheels; a somewhat be-splattered hatch on Q167 offers a clue as to what lies behind. The T-class AEC Regal single-decker dated from December 1929 and had originally been a rear-entrance example, but had been converted to front-entrance format in November 1933.

THIS PAGE

Olympics – Saturday 31 July 1948

Every Christmas from the 1950s until 1978 the Empire Pool, Wembley was the host of a series of spectacular '…On Ice' shows. In front of this venue on 31 July 1948 stood London Transport LTC4 on 'Official Transport' duties for the Olympic games. Based on an AEC 'Renown' chassis, the LTC class had a sliding roof and raised rear seating. Between September 1939 and December 1945, LTC4 was used as a public ambulance. Thereafter, she served as a relief vehicle and so was ideal to be pressed into service for the Games.

Olympics – Saturday 31 July 1948

In 1978 the Empire Pool was rebranded as the Wembley Arena. It was refurbished along with the adjoining stadium and reopened to the public on 2 April 2006 with a concert by Depeche Mode. In 1948 V. C. Jones was also drawn to the foreign buses and coaches parked at Wembley, such as this Volvo B512 coach, a design introduced in 1946. Note how almost all of the cars parked below and left are black.

London Airport – Saturday 31 July 1948

When Pan American World Airways NC88836 *Clipper Mayflower* landed at London Airport in May 1948 it confirmed its role as an international airport. The Lockheed L-049 Constellation was used on the transatlantic route from New York to London via Gander and Shannon, a trip which took some 18 hours. Even so, that represented a vast improvement over the schedule met by ex-military types such as the Avro Lancastrian and Consolidated Liberator, in addition to which the 'Connie' was pressurised.

London – Monday 2 August 1948

Going about his business in London on Monday 2 August 1948, V. C. Jones photographed London Transport RT599 working a relief on Green Line route 706 (London-Tring) at Eccleston Bridge near Victoria. For years the Country Area services had survived on a ragbag of hand-me-downs and 'odds and ends'; however, during July 1948 Tring garage had taken delivery of new RTs, and just a few weeks later their livery of green with cream upper window surrounds and cantrail band was still looking crisp enough to draw the attention of the boys in shorts at right. The now-demolished warehouse belonging to Bishop & Sons Removals formed the background to many a photograph taken of successive generations of Green Line coaches pausing on Eccleston Bridge. RT593, from the same batch of vehicles (although a red bus when new), is now in private preservation.

London – Monday 2 August 1948

Later on in his peregrinations around London on Monday 2 August 1948, V. C. Jones came across Class E/1 tramcar No 1811 derailed at Cedars Road whilst working route 34 – both the pony wheels of the rearmost bogie and the leading wheels of the front bogie are clearly off the rails. Going by the paraphernalia around the kneeling workman, which includes a jack, the tram must have been there for quite a while. It's almost irresistible to suppose that the kneeling man wasn't on the point of saying: "Try her now mate…" The car was built in 1922, withdrawn in October 1951 and scrapped at Penhall Road.

Reading – Sunday 8 August 1948

On Sunday 8 August 1948 the SCTS visited Reading and toured its trolleybus system aboard Corporation trolleybus No 111. At Whitley Street, V. C. Jones hopped off and took a few shots of the vehicle and street scene while the crew looked on. The impressive building at left was a Methodist church, built in 1905. Today it is Reading Hindu Temple & Community Centre.

Reading – Sunday 8 August 1948

Reading had a number of connections with the 1948 Olympics. A separate torch relay was run from Wembley to Torquay – site of the yachting competition. The route from Wembley was: Uxbridge, Slough, Maidenhead, through Reading and then on to Basingstoke, Andover, Salisbury, Sherborne, Yeovil, Exeter and Newton Abbot. The torch was lit in Wembley at 09.00 on Sunday 1 August 1948 and used to light the Torquay Olympic Flame on the balcony of Torre Abbey at 11.00 on Monday 2 August.

The Great Britain Olympic football squad used Elm Park – the home of Reading FC between September 1896 and May 1998 – as its training ground. The team included Reading's Bill Amor, who only played in the Third Place (bronze medal) play off match on 13 August 1948, which ended in defeat and so he did not receive a medal. He did however score a goal – Great Britain's third and last in the match – making him the only Reading player to do so at an Olympic games.

Transport arrangements for the rowing events at Henley had proved very difficult to organise. Competitors were housed in four centres in High Wycombe, thirteen miles distant. During the early days of the Games their training programme continued unabated, but London Transport could not spare extra buses during the critical early morning hours. So local firms, including ones in Reading, supplied luxury coaches to augment the fleet. The Reading organisation provided an experienced official to who was delegated the task of running the High Wycombe-Henley coach service, which was augmented by two Ministry of Supply station wagons. Coaches were ordered on a daily hire and contract mileage basis of 120 miles per day per vehicle.

Reading Corporation introduced its trolleybus service to Whitley on 18 July 1936. Although the new vehicles led to a 43% increase in passengers, they were not popular with everyone here in Whitley Street. Some had relied on the noise of the trams they replaced to wake them up in the morning – something the near-silent trolleybuses singularly failed to do! In this front ¾ view, V. C. Jones also caught the serried rows of houses beyond the Methodist Chapel. The advert on the bus side is for Jackson's Outfitters, which was founded on 17 September 1875 by Edward Jackson. Its Jackson's Corner store is still a notable feature of the town.

Reading – Sunday 8 August 1948

Reading Corporation trolleybus No 111 had an AEC 661T chassis and a Park Royal body seating 30 upstairs and 26 downstairs. It was placed in traffic on 21 May 1939 and remained in service until 5 September 1961. An SCTS 'RESERVED' label can clearly be seen at the bottom right of the windscreen. An extension to Whitley Wood was implemented on 7 August 1949, but this closed on 8 January 1967, to be followed on 3 November 1968 by the remainder of the route.

An Olympic Summer

Reading – Sunday 8 August 1948

Trolleybus overhead required almost continual maintenance; essential for this purpose were specially adapted vehicles like Reading Corporation Commer Superpoise tower wagon No 33, new in July 1946 and still extant in preservation today. Above the cab was an elevating platform, which provided a safe working environment for the crew performing these vital duties. The tag on the overhead behind the tower wagon indicated the point that required attention..

London – Kennington Gate – Sunday 15 August 1948

Walking around London on Sunday 15 August 1948, V. C. Jones took this shot of trams in Kennington Park Road. Oval underground station can be seen at left, and on the extreme left is a temporary road sign for Wembley put up for the Olympics, which had finished the day before. This, like much else to do with the games, would soon be taken down and packed away, as the two weeks of the Olympics quickly receded in people's memories. Note also the sales barrow outside the station, once a common sight on London's streets. Harleyford Street runs between the station and the flats to the left, whilst Camberwell New Road swings off to the right, beyond the gates to St Mark's Church.

London – *Passport to Pimlico* set – Sunday 15 August 1948

The Ealing Studios film Passport to Pimlico was not made in Pimlico, but about a mile away, on the other side of the River Thames, where a huge set was built on a cleared bombsite on the Lambeth Road and the corner of Hercules Road. Seen here from the latter, one of the studio staff speaks to interested passers-by, whilst a tram passes by along Lambeth Road. The film's story – of respite from a ration-laden Britain through the accidental discovery that Pimlico was part of ration-free Burgundy – offered a fleeting and vicarious escape from the reality of a slow recovery from war, which, for some, the Olympics had also given briefly. The area has now been totally redeveloped, but by standing on the Lambeth Road between Hercules Road and Kennington Road and looking north toward Lambeth Bridge, one can still recognise the railway arches that dominated the set.

London Underground – Saturday 21 August 1948

On Saturday 21 August 1948 V. C. Jones photographed trains at Golders Green station on the Northern Line. The station was built by the Charing Cross, Euston & Hampstead Railway and opened on 22 June 1907. It was one of that railway's two northern terminals (with Archway) and also the site of its depot. The departing train is comprised of 1938 tube stock, built by Metro-Cammell and the Birmingham Railway Carriage & Wagon Co. This stock was used on London Underground until 1988, working on the Bakerloo, Central, East London, Northern and Piccadilly lines.

London Underground – Saturday 21 August 1948

To the south of Golders Green station, in the tunnels beneath Hampstead Heath (at extreme left) – is the partially built but uncompleted North End, or Bull & Bush station. Plans were made before World War 1 to extend the line north from Golders Green to Hendon and Edgware,

but the war postponed this work and it did not begin until 12 June 1922. The extension's first section, to Hendon Central, opened on 19 November 1923. Here a Morden-bound train of 1938 stock enters Golders Green.

London – Saturday 21 August 1948

As an eventful summer progressed there were signs of optimism, fostered by the success of the Olympics.
Still, here and there, reminders remained of the work that still lay ahead. At Bromley-by-Bow V. C. Jones caught
a turning STL1853 on route 108A showing Rochester Way, while behind another STL is a bomb-damaged school –
legacy of a conflict whose repercussions would take many more years to resolve.